In Baltic Circles

In Baltic Circles

Paul Violi

H_NGM_N BKS
REISSUES
www.h-ngm-nbks.com

FIRST H_NGM_N REISSUES EDITION, OCTOBER 2011

ISBN 978-0-9832215-3-1

Cover portrait by Paula North, taken from the original
edition published by Kulchur Foundation in 1973.

Book and cover design by Eric Appleby

For additional material on Paul Violi and *In Baltic Circles*, please visit
www.h-ngm-n.com/in-baltic-circles

Biographical Note

Paul Violi wrote eleven books of poetry in his lifetime (plus two chapbooks that he tended not to include in his publications list), including *Overnight*, *Fracas*, *The Curious Builder*, and *Likewise* from Hanging Loose Press. A selection of his longer poems, *Breakers*, was issued by Coffee House Press. Widely published and anthologized both in the U.S. and abroad, he received two National Endowment for the Arts fellowships in poetry, as well as grants from the Ingram Merrill Foundation, The New York Foundation for the Arts, the Fund for Poetry, The Foundation for Contemporary Arts, and a John Ciardi Lifetime Achievement Award. In 2001 he received The Morton Dauwen Zabel Award from the American Academy of Arts and Letters.

Born in New York in 1944, Violi grew up in Greenlawn, Long Island, and graduated from Boston University with a B.A. in English and a minor in Art History. After a stint in the Peace Corps doing map completion and survey work in northern Nigeria, Violi traveled extensively through Africa, Europe and Asia. Upon returning to New York he worked for WCBS-TV, then for various newspapers and magazines. He was managing editor of *The Architectural Forum* from 1972–1974 and worked on freelance projects at Universal Limited Art Editions, researching correspondence of poets and artists and assisting Buckminster Fuller while he wrote the text of *Tetrascroll*. As chairman of the Associate Council Poetry Committee, Violi organized various reading series at the Museum of Modern Art from 1974 to 1983. He also co-founded Swollen Magpie Press, which produced poetry chapbooks, the poets and painters anthology *Broadway*— edited by James Schuyler and Charles North—and a poetry magazine called *New York Times*.

Waterworks, a short selection of his early poems from Toothpaste Press, appeared in 1972, and Kulchur Foundation brought out *In Baltic Circles* the following year. Bill Zavatsky's Sun Press published two of Violi's books, *Harmatan*, a long poem set in Nigeria, in 1977 and *Splurge* in 1981. In 1993 he curated an exhibit "Kenneth Koch: Collaborations with Artists" for Christchurch Mansion, Ipswich, U.K., and his art-book collaborations with Dale Devereux Barker, most recently *Envoy; Life is Completely Interesting*, have been acquired by many libraries and museums. The expanded text of their first collaboration, *Selected Accidents, Pointless Anecdotes*, a collection of non-fiction prose, was published by Hanging Loose in 2002.

Violi taught at various colleges, universities, and other institutions, both public and private, including New York University, The Dalton School, Sing Sing, Stevens Institute of Technology, Bloomfield College, State University of New York at Purchase, and Scarsdale Teachers Institute. At the time of his death in April of 2011 he was teaching in the Department of English and Comparative Literature at Columbia University and in the graduate writing program at New School University.

Editorial Acknowledgments

In Baltic Circles was first published in 1973 by Kulchur Foundation.

The editors would like to thank the following people without whom this reissue would not have been possible: Paul and Ann Violi, Tony Towle, Charles and Paula North, Amanda Smeltz, Liz Hildreth, and Eric Appleby.

We'd also like to thank Jeremy Schmall and Justin Taylor, editors of *The Agriculture Reader* and Michael Schiavo, editor of *Gondola*, for reprinting some of these poems in advance of this publication.

Before passing away in April, 2011, Paul Violi was directly involved in the editing and proofreading of this reissue. Any differences between this version and the original represent corrections or changes that were expressly requested by the author himself.

Cover portrait by Paula North
Book and cover design by Eric Appleby
Introduction by Nate Pritts
Afterword by Matt Hart

Contents

Introduction

by Nate Pritts

Paul Violi's poems burst with wild energy, put incorrigibly in the service of a no-holds-barred aesthetic that makes his poetry happen everywhere. Though there can be great, good fun in Violi's work, there is also the pathos of the flipside; along with his bombastic slapstick caricatures, & truly revelated language, comes a capacity for the most tender human emotions, the most delicate linguistic touches. This makes sense—few writers match Violi's ability to give reign to unfettered emotion, playfulness & love, which necessarily gives rise to the possibility for disappointment, frustration, & remorse.

In Baltic Circles was Violi's first full-length collection, released by the Kulchur Foundation in 1973. *Kulchur*, the magazine, lasted 20 issues, & the press brought out such important & resounding books as Ted Berrigan & Ron Padgett's *Bean Spasms* (1967), David Antin's *Talking* (1972) & Joseph Ceravolo's *Millennium Dust* (1982), among many others. Founded by Marc Schleifer in 1961, he would soon thereafter & forevermore cede control to Lita Hornick who served as primary editor & driving force. Sadly, Violi's book is now close to impossible to find.

The H_NGM_N BKS Reissues series started with the aim of bringing important & vital literary texts back into our contemporary conversation & we continue that with the reissue of *In Baltic Circles*. In a publishing culture that seems ever more fixated on bringing readers the newest iteration, I think it's important to keep our eyes on our roots. It is my hope that by making this book available again, new & return readers can joyously remember that the antidote to indifference is zany generosity, to counter detachment with a limitless range of feeling.

In Baltic Circles

Paul Violi

Acknowledgments

Some of these poems first appeared in the following publications: *The American Poetry Review*, *The East Village Other*, *The Herald*, *New York Times*, *Telephone*, *Third Assembling*, *Gum*, *The Harris Review*, *Extensions*, *Penumbra*, *Blue Suede Shoes*, *Toothpaste*, *Mulberry*, *One*, *Matchbook*, *Chapbook*, *Connections*, *Strange Faeces*, *Sun*, *Sunshine*, *The World*, *Intrepid*, *Roy Rogers*, *Mouth*, *Search for Tomorrow*, *Some*, *Fourth Assembling*, *The Milk Quarterly*.

And in the earlier collections: *She'll Be Riding Six White Horses* (Swollen Magpie Press, 1970); *Automatic Transmissions* (Swollen Magpie Press, 1970); *Waterworks* (Toothpaste Press, 1972).

Cover by Paula North

for Charles North and Tony Towle

PUBLIC WORKS

Swinburne pulls up to the light
with 35 screeching yellow cabs.
They rev their engines
the light turns red
they sound their horns
and off they go.

"Tally ho," yells Swinburne, "tally ho!"

Monet crosses the George Washington Bridge
without thinking about
our first President's dentures.
He could care less.
He drives slowly up the Palisades.
A flock of cabs passed him a long time ago.
It's 11:63 a.m. and he could care less.
It's a warm spring day
and the bugs splatter like snowflakes
against his windshield.
Soon it is covered with the multi-colored splotches.
He stops for gas.
When the attendant begins to clean the windshield
Monet can do one of two things: he either

(Hi, I'm Paul Violi and I'd like a word with you
about BIC pens. I've written some swell poems
with BIC pens and so has my wife, Ann. I expect
our child will really like BIC pens too. You know

how ordinary pens sometimes botch things up and
give you a glimpse of things to come like, well,
when I'm old and getting a bit, uh, senile, I suppose
my mind, like yours, neighbor, will skip a word
here and there, scratch a mere impression of what
should have been a fine thought on the page and,
in a manner of speaking, just plain run out of ink.
But there is no reason your pen has to falter like
that and you can bet BIC pens never will. So take
my advice, do yourself a favor and buy a BIC pen
today. Pick up a couple for the whole family while
you're at it and tell them I sent you!)

It's still a warm spring day
and a man waving
a square orange flag
diverts Monet into the outer lane.

Other men in red vests
have placed orange stanchions in the road,
another drives a blue truck at 3 miles per hour.
They follow him on foot, spraying white lines
and double white lines, yellow lines
and broken yellow lines while 3 men in black boots
chop up shiny casks of tar, melt it
and scribble the stuff over the cracks
in the pavement.
The gray concrete sparkles and its reflection hovers
over it like a mirage on the wrong road to wonderland.

The first to eat lunch
wipes his hands on a green T-shirt.

He steps off the road and examines a tomato
and cheese sandwich: ". . . I remember a job
we did near the shore, a parking lot.
My brother Harry worked that one.
So did my cousin and my nephew.
We laid down about an acre of asphalt
near the beach and I used to take my daughter
there at odd hours for driving lessons.

I explained to her how we had put down
a long white line and then angling into that one
a lot of short, slanted ones.
But she said it looked like the skeleton of a fish.
I couldn't teach her anything.
She lives in the city now. I think she's married.

But in the summer, it's packed on Sundays
and let me tell you something: when I see all the spaces
filled and the cars glittering like a fish on its side
in the sunlight, I want to tell you
it's no accident. I'm glad my brother convinced me
to take this job. It ain't all politics."

The rest of the men unpack their lunches.
Some exchange sandwiches, some of them drink orange
soda, others guzzle grape juice or beer.

The second crew has finished shoveling asphalt
off the back of the truck.
The paint is still drying,
all the holes in the road are now bumps.

OF ANN

You, among changes

     in a sunless purple sky that's either
the dawn or twilight

     an orange   an empty glass

on the table near the birches

as the leaves surface to the day
or the trees deepen, peaceably, darker than the night.

You, within your thoughts

     enclose as many openings

as a flower, white and nurtured
by the edge that solitude shares with change.

SONNET FOR
THE EARL OF SURREY

The golfer smiles in his polo shirt, the little
man has beaten the bully, the housewife is
using a new detergent and the Californian squints
behind his sunglasses; the man in the diner likes
his new bow tie and so does the doctor who saved
the injured cheerleader; the detective uses hair
tonic, the stout nurse is immaculate, the waitress
wants to date the truckdriver; the grocer slices
a pound of baloney, the reporter asks him how it
feels; the teacher wears a wild shirt, the coach
tells the youngster to shape up or ship out, the old
lady asks him the time, the woman in curlers orders
a hamburger and yet I want to jump for joy.

TANKA

Fallen moths

    fluttering on the surface

       of the pond

O Cremora

Why have you come back

TO CISCO IN THE SWAMPS

Translated from
Ada Cisco Indentro Las Zwompas
by Wolfram de Zorro

Cisco, my old companion,
They tell me you are wandering now,
That you have given all your possessions
To the Sisters of The Purple Charity,
    the Sisters who wear the spurs.

They say you play in the muck
And your mind has abandoned your eyes,
That you just look at people when they talk
And scratch yourself and smile
As if you were arguing with the sun.

Does this mean the air itself no longer hesitates
When the Muse cranks your mind
And your thoughts are no longer swift and clean
As the slot machine,
And the pictures never coincide
So the words, nay, silver coins
    can pour forth from your lips?

I hear you have seen your own soul
And described it not as the green ball
The Gypsies fear (Gypsy's sphere!)
But as a furtive, impoverished twerp

That hangs around you as if you were
A dying man with 300 ducats in your purse.

Cisco, they tell me, Wolfram de Zorro,
That we will never again whet our swords
On the hearts of the Austrians,
Nor go wenching together in Mantua or Grenola,
Nor roam the streets at dawn
Smacking the parking meters to have the coins
Spill into our hands like the advice of prophets.

Cisco, if you don't reply by the Candlemas Feast,
I shall know you have drunk your coffee
And seen your reflection in the bottom of the cup.
Henceforth, the missions to the Low Countries
Will all be uphill and although your songs
Will still sparkle like my horses' hoofs,
You will be less than the dust on their teeth.

CHANGES

Walking home on 57th Street

A mood extended in the dampness,
an inner sky
in which remembrance coincides with faces
pressed against steamy windows.

Cars and buses pass,
their tires unwinding opaque tracks,
visual echoes of my thoughts that fade back
                    into the shiny asphalt.

The snow became rain,
the rain a mist; the motion itself—a film
of memories formed and lost,
of how the difference between Keats'
and Shelley's epitaphs becomes fused in my mind.

Mizzle to mist, shades of a process
into which words immediately dissolve
                after striving, on a clearer day,
                    as if I were the wind, the water
                        that I could speak what is happening.

MARCH

Sometimes I feel it's all wrong
and the spoiler has been in his biplane
                    writing the word BLUE
across an immaculate sky,
   but now everything seems to cohere—
      cast your net like sunlight on the water.

Each day's been riding the crest of the week,
these streets are made for coasting,
for idleness and amazement,
for acknowledging the cheers of welcoming crowds
or sitting down next to stone lions in the sun.

Flip a pebble and again ripples vibrate
through the pool, resounding
from the park to the café,
          to the circular, intervolved stains
left by cups and saucers on the bare wooden table;
   a course remains: elemental shapes that confide
in the transparent confusion of space and time,
   figures of the wind in the dance of the mind.

NICEAN

Last month, the moon reduced to the inane grin
of an old lady who used to sing for the troops.

Tonight, I'm in the grass, I suppose; feeling
  I've always been here
        waiting and thinking
  about what the wind shapes to its mood:
ancient prospects ride the airwaves,
arctic sabbaths and clouds from other famous
       but extinguished secrets.
I'm thinking about what the wind shapes to its
mood and you arrive without distracting me.

    The moon is full of lies, maybe
the water enjoys listening to them; the snow
  believes them and melts,

It is another way of seeing
  and it surprises me with your scalp, your
thighs, your throat; I've always wanted a map
which changes as I follow it.

Soon we are gladly lost,
    your fingernails coolly tracing the confusion.
      The wind shifts
and the sunken galleons have risen to the day
    encrusted with coral and shells.

No one has ever suspected they would, but here they are
      and their captains are drunk.

It's midnight and the moon is full of praise.
      The wine is gone and the tropical sky
blooms with the parachutes of a thousand assassins
      who'll effortlessly drown in the sea.

SLEEPING DACTYLS
AND LURKING IAMBS

When I think how our love has been
slow and often tumultuous
like the process facing those who
want to radicalize public
housing management, I never
doubt its ultimate success will
have a very heavy impact.
Most especially if we work at it.

Just as these new urban poor will
be incorporated in the mainstream
of life, we will witness slight but
meaningful and lasting changes
which will reach a high level of involvement
as the exciting developments unfold.

INTERVALE

Nightcloud with the moon behind her

Winter beach
and boats
      turned over on the sand

Does sand: provoke you
                      bore you
                      curiously disappoint you
                      all of the above

I wish you would hurry

. . . knowing what to expect
and yet be surprised
                (sails suddenly caught
                    in the wind)

We should always wait for each other
        in a wide-open place

thinking about the silver
the moon gains with distance

and how the awkwardness of the gulls,
        perched nearby,

is dispelled
once they've taken flight

. . . the extent between us now
forming a sky
for the moment you arrive

THE CHRONICLES
OF A SPACE CADET

for Charles and Paula North

Rapids in moonlight   their banzai anthems

" . . . the water awakes and travels
            on its imagination for a while."

In The Chronicles of Wule,
it is said the fish smile
in the faster currents.

I have read The Chronicles of Wule, twice,
and this is my report: the author
sought in remoteness
an immunity that was finally more
than the sound of rain could cure.

The initial passages are remarkably intelligible
and pleasing, as a fine and steady rain
is to someone who waits for empty trains
and always wanted to learn Japanese.

He earned a decent living, we have proof of this,
and managed to support a family of five; each child
a spaniel-eyed enlargement of the next.

After too many empty trains passed him by,
his children took him here: a cabin

overlooking the rapids, cupboards stacked
with canned goods and a lot of property;
wandering around, he would get lost
in the snow and pines like a flea
in the starkness of his own scalp.

Out of his indiscriminate research, came
the word Wule. It belongs
to an Upper Gambian dialect and denotes
a grievous and disabling state of self-pity
that translates as either "hot rain"
or "someone who wears his asshole for a necklace."

"The nights were black as carbon paper
and [these are not my words] the days
were exact copies of all the rest."

There were attempts at revival: the best
parts of The Chronicles
are an account of his toting
a steaming basket of laundry
out into the yard one cold afternoon;
the most desperate entry describes his failure
to cope with a pair of frozen dungarees.

Revelry, singed whiskers, unmitigated realism:
the fish he writes of never close their eyes.
Chapters end with him stolid, speechless,
facing sunlit shores and chewing cellophane.

Weather, metastasis, emotions served with
meteorological spoons: paragraphs

in which the black and blue sky swarms
over trampled cornfields and the chubby women
there who undress and laugh; some of them
have gold teeth, they all play the tuba.

Ardor, high voltage antics, but eventually
the expanse he called "smithereens"
where his Chronicles lingered like Arabic,
almost legible messages that disappeared
as his musical cigarette smoke
scrawled them in the air.

Sheets draped over the furnishings
of houses, shrubs and parked cars covered
with a heavy snowfall: his celebrations
are sequestered in the death of suburbia
or startling March days that surrounded him
with flurries of snow
that never reached the ground,
as once, strolling across a bridge,
he stopped: "at the height of a splendid obscurity"
from where he could still see the leaves
carried on the rippled hide of the river
a hundred feet below while the flakes
scurried before his eyes like memories
in the mind of someone
who is rapidly going blind.

EXCERPTS FROM
THE CHRONICLES

My tooth aches and a drowsy numbness pains
   my head; the gas the dentist gave me
sent me soaring through a pinhole in the sky
   It was, to my estimation, Zero Hour

****

Throwing books out of high windows
         only to see them descend again
later, as I sit under the lamp
   and the wasted moths fall into my lap

It's a difficult habit to break

****

Planes lost in the fog, monotonous lullabies,
They'll drone on for a while, they'll sputter
and crash and briefly disturb the crickets

but then, my white hour, we will finally sleep

****

A housing development continues its glacial
movement through the hills
Impossibilities flounder on the opposite horizon

. . . yank the paper out of the typewriter, crumple
it up, toss it on the floor
The cat pounces, struts away triumphantly holding
the paper in its mouth like a bird

****

In a large, unfurnished sunlit room
a man nails an extraordinary book to the floor

****

I went to my favorite restaurant
and ordered a typewriter
While I typed I watched this typewriter
eat corn off the cob

****

O hollow autumn skies rusty madness
fumes of red voyages down wooden streets

Your clowns bore me
The exhausted women in the willow trees
have thrown their costumes under the setting sun
I don't believe in the benefits of an eight hour sleep
I will prolong this fatigue as long as possible
Chaos will wear my composure like a wound
The wind will polish my nose

****

There is a fly in the room
with a reward on its head
Heinrich Himmler looked like a fly
No, Joseph Goebbels looked like a fly
Heinrich Himmler looked like a bookworm

****

You klutz, you can't scribble without drawing a pile of rope .

****

The radio announcer finished playing his selection
and addressed the panel.
    Dr. Sandler was convinced the music was an early
    concerto by Haydn.
    Dr. Salmaggio doubted this very much but tended
    to agree.
    Dr. Winetz scoffed at these speculations: "All
of what you say is mere words, he protested, I have
no respect for them whatsoever, they are much
too subservient to your thoughts!"
    I, myself, found the discussion worthwhile
but couldn't give it the attention it undoubtedly
deserved and continued shuffling through the house,
pants down around my ankles, searching for toilet paper.

****

The nights were as black as carbon paper
and the days
were exact copies of all the rest.

****

Notice

This elevator is not working today.
Just consider it an anonymous eulogy.
Please use the 53rd Street entrance.
Thank you for your cooperation—

The Management

from THE CAMPAIGN JOURNALS

It was the first time I'd seen the intrepid general falter. Fiorvante's decoded message shook in his shaking hand. Squinting with agitation, my leader tried to regain that famous concentration which had mastered many a maelstrom of distress. His spirits had to be rejuvenated and, remembering how terms of venery delighted him, I pointed to the dastardly message with my riding crop and then contributed: "It's all a crock of shit, Sir!"

But it was no use, I doubt whether he heard me. Fiorvante was surrounded and Tzara's troops were assaulting the left flank. Confused, worried, the good man's countenance enacted his anxiety as the chance of victory seemed more and more remote: his thick eyebrows resembled two black caterpillars trying to get around each other on the same branch.

FREE LEADERSHIP SAMPLE

You never know when things will get serious.
One should keep certain lines at hand
(like a dime for a pay toilet)
for the moment when somebody
will have to say something.
So tear along the perforation
for this Free Leadership Sample:

....

Brothers! we are like snowflakes—
alone we dissolve on a pebble;
together we can change the course of rivers!

SCHMIDT
or
THE UNFORTUNATE TRAVELER

Schmidt resides in a remote, mountainous hotel whose neon name glimmers indecipherably in the smog. This solemn establishment sits at the end of a yellow promenade that once led to the sun. Every tenant there has signed a petition requesting that he be immediately evicted. All day, Schmidt sits in his window, dimly glowing like the pupil in a destitute jeweler's only eye. And on a shelf by that solitary window is a bottle filled with smoke and labeled: "my illness." It is regrettable, perhaps, that any further revelations concerning this man's circumstances are prohibited while he and members of his family are still alive. He shall surely remain an enigma to his countrymen and former associates. Meanwhile, gulls cavort above the brick chimney, whirling and diving in spirals through a diminishing cloud of steam, as the laws of mutability clear the air, preparing us for a little razzmatazz, for the appearance of yet unimagined things whose emergence in our skies, it may be fair to assume, will be viewed from their former dimension as a demise.

EXTRACT

. . . despite his protestations, his crew drank of the fountain and forever afterwards the history of Sardinia had one wet page. He waited until a raincloud passed over the island and set out after it, alone, hoisting the sail up the mast, brushing the spiders off his shoulders and arms as they tumbled sleepily out of the unfurling canvas.

For three weeks, the water, entranced by the brilliance of the sun, didn't move. As his plight worsened, he ate a shoe. He beat out his misery on the ocean with a paddle. He ate another shoe.

Then one night, eyes rusty from lack of sleep, he espied a silver ark nearing the horizon; descending so leisurely it could have been the half moon that was up there the night before. Swiftly he rowed and swiftly he climbed aboard; naked girls with green eyes and soft necks, with thighs that whispered as they walked, comforted him with plums and wine and wiped his brow with lemon peels.

The vessel was propelled by the beauty of their songs and they sang all the way to the yellow sun and blue mountains of France.

Throughout the journey, his dreams never changed with the geography. But, once ashore, his sleep was no longer troubled by the shitty little creatures that breathed smoke and farted ashes and whined under the willows at night like oblivion's gray flames.

Exploring the countryside, he entertained the natives who marveled at what he showed them: a mirror which transformed every noogal into a lagoon; the circular horns of a shaggy goat; and a bug he called wasp, explaining to the people how it was created by a Japanese man out of black ink and a little brushwork.

And lo, they marveled when they heard of metallic utensils for eating and the location of Buddha's footprint, of a land where water was married to rock, and a place where poems had no inside or outside but were stuffed into the ears of the dead.

And they sighed when he told them he knew the cause of the common cold but that to reveal it would cause millions of people grave embarrassment and far more discomfort than the illness itself.

He recounted his trials and travails in the dominion of Uz where the inhabitants were consigned with the dinosaurs to a state of perpetual infancy and the lizards stretched their necks all day, futilely prodding the stagnant skies.

As he spoke the memory of Elemenopee, the princess who helped rescue him, filled his head with a resonant sunlight that filled her palace, slanting down through the venetian blinds like slices of angels fallen through harps from great heights.

He talked no more, allowing his tale to tell itself, moving amid the white furniture of an audience's imagination where a mortal's words would sink with the weight of disbelief.

They saw how he, a strayed reveler, disguised himself as a mathematician whose life and theories had culminated in a terminal euphoria, and thereby confounded the banshees which had been pursuing him.

A dazzled mule then appeared hauling a wagon full of grapes along a circular conception of time. He rode on the back, his head resting on a pillow stuffed with frozen feathers as the mule sniffed the sound of Elemenopee's flute, a yurthful wurvering and gliding, a melody that attracted so many grackles, juncos and jays as to darken the idle skies and cause the weather to be moved once by a memory of the future and remain forever unpredictable and lost to itself.

VALEDICTION

(profference up to the wild blue yonder,
a few practice sessions:

).

BEGIN—
    a lake flattered by a breeze

    and so, with a final, steady breath
    the water rising to a bubble
         and gingerly carried away

PENSIONE

Rome '67

Follow through the night the round street lamps
that line the Tiber's curve like photographs
depicting the phases of the moon
and return and wait again
fanned by the clock in numbered rooms
while the fly beats itself senseless
against the window pane
and the night turns the glass into a mirror.

Frightened by her age.
Shaved crotch. Abortion?
No, she lied, the Arab liked her that way.
The Arab didn't like her any way

Melancholia.
She grieved for more moons,
for Jupiter nights,
for something other than a day;
she plotted the shores of Atlantis
along the cracked and peeling walls,
the footsteps she heard
parodied the life she had led
as skinny old men
followed tired whores down the halls.

Cigarette smoke curling in the dank air,
the earth spinning into a cocoon:

Take care

Will you be around in the spring . . . ?

SUMMER

Spent some of the day
   holding a toad
spheres for eyes, black and gold.

Then put up the sheet-rock and spackled
it with Myron, who showed up
   drunk every morning,
fired five times that week
   except Saturday,
everyone's drunk on Saturday.

Seth, a friend of his, took the precaution
of nailing his shoes to the scaffold
so when he fell he never hit the ground.

   . . . looked up later
to see him saw himself right off the roof.

60 years old. Carpenter.
3 dollars per hour. 1 black tooth in his mouth.

Old handmade nails and spikes,
    the planks pried up
       mephitic air.

   Surface of the floorboards rock hard
but the bottom rotten
grown back into the ground.

More planks pried up, innumerable insects
             frantic in the light.

And grimy, swearing workers
   walking away,
       hatched from the torn-down shed.

ON THE RISE

East on 7th Street
like portraits, dusty oils, an old immigrant
sitting behind each window

White monster garbage truck
grinds up yesterday

   grim tramp in the alley
   rummaging through cans
    drops a scrap into his burlap bag
     and totters away

     Sway-back Pegasus
moseying over toward the park
    and a few spades
bopping locomotive
motherfucker-motherfucker-motherfucker

But the street a stream
     Mira! Mira!
kids dragging their girlfriends
into the open priapic hydrants

East clouds over the hot day
smell of moisture in the air
and suddenly trees
anxious and lively
    below the imminent rain

include girls dancing
and a muffled rock beat

long hair tossing

saying climb on me

saying
welcome to the sky

HAROLD AND IMOGENE

The beautiful Imogene is finally alone
with him. She wants to tell him she knows
he is a Martian but that she also loves
him and his secret is safe with her.
As he turns and hands her her drink she blurts
out her confession, throwing her arms
around his neck. His response petrifies her.
He becomes totally rigid. A horrible
realization stuns her to sobriety. She mumbles
the words before they are formed in her mind:
"You come from another galaxy, don't you?
You're probably different from us, aren't you?
You've been transformed to look like us, haven't you?
Why for all I know, I'm repulsive to you!"
She faints. Harold knows she will tell the other
house guests that he is secretly a Martian
and endanger the success of his mission.
He knows what he must do. He unclasps
the cuff-link that contains a vial of de-metabolizing
fluid. He drops it. It shatters on the floor.
Panicked, he gets down and starts licking the fluid
off the tile. It is a futile exercise.
Something else stops him, however. He has noticed
his reflection on the shiny surface. Imogene,
that very afternoon, had waxed those tiles
with SUPER BRITE, the all-new floor wax
that is the nation's leading seller.
Harold stares at his gleaming visage.

He realizes he will be wearing that mask
for the rest of his mortal days on planet Earth.
His dejection is profound. He stands up, knocks
his head against the mantelpiece and sobs.

L

British Honduras is more advanced than Honduras.
Red flowers already bloomed on the plum trees.
Moles, burrowing further in their search for sleep,
have reached the lawns of the Presidential Palace.
The girls in the short skirts paid their checks
and walked all the way across the plaza
before the impression of the wicker seats
faded from the backs of their thighs.
For over three months the beaches have been deserted.
Those of us who went for a swim
and forgot to remove our glasses
lost them in the surf, and after looking
awhile returned by a more distant road
to the highlands; the lenses must be worn away
by now, waves pouring through the hollow frames.
It rained for 28 days in June, more
days than reported anywhere else.
5 more than in Honduras.
Since then, the sky stalled, clear and blue,
and left the crops, the corn and tomato plants,
sulking in the heat, sunflowers bent to the ground.
The wind alone could tell you all this,
for you would be the first to notice
how the sound of it brushing the eucalyptus
changes as the leaves become more dry.
Numerous visitors arrive on the evening ship.
The prospect of unimpeded freedom and relaxation
has made us more sedentary, content to lie

in the grass and read, letting the wind turn the pages.
We can see a little further every day,
further than anyone could ever see in Honduras.
Sleep's black chandeliers remain lit
for a few convenient moments
until we are fully awake and the maid has entered
the room and opened the louvered shutters.
But as the horizon widens with each morning,
so does the complaisance of this country
a complaisance that in Honduras would be dangerous.
But not here. It will undoubtedly get worse
yet result in a tedium that under our skies
is expected to bloom into a monstrous orchid.
At least, this is the belief quite popular
among the people I'm acquainted with in the city.
And I think it admirable, considering
the edges of next year are already in view
and clearly rough times are in store for them,
rougher times than anyone in Honduras can imagine:
our artists' newest murals depict a squandered
city full of mules chewing on white violins;
or deserts sunk in the same silence
with which the Atlantic swells:
hardened ground littered with seashells,
broken red rocks, pages of books
on which nothing is left but the punctuation.
Strangers in cowls stop to watch anyone
who walks out to the end of the dunes.
And after a while, their stares, though still impolite,
manage to penetrate the interminable daylight
that serves each hour on an empty plate.
But opposing all this, I have my own picture,

praised by some critics for its "distant immediacy"
and more valuable than any picture in Honduras.
It shows the glass boats that drift between the stars
and the city that shines darkly in your eyes:
a permanent place, the tables full,
the people omniscient yet easily surprised.

ANTIGUA

wet grass wiping against our

On the way down to

say, into, the　　　first night here

"damn thorns" until

impressions in the sand

Something born there

an egg splitting in the sunlight)

Something

that began eating its shell
staggered around

at night, beating itself into

wings

and up, into

a cloud swallows the moon

MYSTERIOUS BLURB WITH DOTS

Aging, suffering from neglect, the Liberian liner, named after a mythological Hindu deity, heads East toward Singapore carrying all aboard into the most shattering adventure of their tumultuous lives . . . .

Tornetta

a desperate murderer fleeing from a professional executioner who may also be aboard the vessel . . . .

The Gurstons

a haunted family running from the memories of a grisly tragedy . . . .

Melina

beautiful, bisexual, and self-degrading, in dire need of kindness and love . . . .

Donovan

the ship's doctor, cool and self-possessed, but faced—in one violent moment—with the greatest trial of his career . . . .

From the start, they and others like them brought a web of conflict to the ship that finally caught them in an inexorable maze. . . . but it would take one of the most hair-raising experiences in modern literature to decide who would survive and who wouldn't. . . . . . .

EQUATORIAL

(Actuality)
   "says the smile
of Good-Humour-Man-Walking-Over-Moss."
Actualities that would fade with explanations.
He comes downstream quite often.
His advice is cherished by the Riverfolk
and has usurped the local currency:

     Stupidity is the ability to repeat mistakes.

     Why don't you Saskatchewan.

     Why don't you Sparrow.

But the Islanders never heard of him.
For years their demise was observed from the shore
as water eroded the embankments,
landslides tumbled into the river
and illusions collapsed in their minds.
Yet, Good-Humour-Man-Walking-Over-Moss
kept yelling at them up to the final bubble:

     Present Tense!

     Fly a kite!

     Climb it!

Ack-Ack!

Octoroon!

Catch Fire!

A luminescent epitaph, alack, appeared offshore
on a buoy, and the inscription read:

"They Squat Too Close To The Wall"

. . . The Riverfolk visit the Pine grove
after it rains. They'll Be there,
looking up through the
                    Tarmac
                    Balsam
                    and Fir

and then leave when the needles
and branches forget a brilliant vagary and dry.

Usually, places like that are referred to
with the name of one of their daughters,
not so much as a designation
but to commend an aspect of time;
it would be known as Juliana
if her name were Julia,
or Carolina if her name were Carole, and so on.
They always speak of two things at once.
That's all I'm going to say.

PROGRESSION

She kissed me
She should have waited
until
I'd taken the cigarette
out of my mouth

But then . . . the ashes on her lips

SUBTERRANEAN

It's going to be a bad day. After 10 and
can't even see the sun.
Woke up suspicious
with every hair on my head hurting.
Woke down
        and started off in third gear.
I'm positive it's going to be a bad day;
if it's four feet down, I'll fall five.
Grimy mattress. sheets. and soot
from dreams of tigers
        born leaping through fiery hoops.

Sleep fled when daylight, wearing a tyrannical boot,
kicked a dog to see if it were asleep or dead.
It woke up and died.

IDLEWILD

for Ann

A feather just flew in the window
    Celebration!
    a barrage of compliments
for whoever is balling or making music,
working at what they know best
        or just feels like smiling
  Wind blowing this way
nudging the trees to surge
        so the leaves rise and applaud
and a sweep of rain hits the glistening pavement
  with a thousand exclamation points

Lightning trying to grab the earth,
    joyful women run for cover
breasts bobbling under wet blouses,
   roaches scramble through the kitchen
the window sill covered with pigeon droppings
        and signed—Seurat
  One thought generating another
the momentum growing until the mind
    spins sweetly like a top

And here comes the sun
and two girls
      both beautiful and arrogant
      both wearing spats
   striped double-breasted suits

and broad-brim hats,
　　　　strolling along arm in arm
　　　　　　so cool
in the crystal aftermath
where things surprise each other
　　　　and feel good together
　　　like roses and coal
　　　　　and water flowing over chrome.

TORN AND FRAYED

The famous Boston Goddess:
sacred snakes encircle her wrists,
the right arm is restored
but her hands are ancient;
collar, nipples and corsage are gold.

A bearded cloaked and booted reveler
stoops to raise a bowl of wine.
A boy plays double flutes.

A young girl standing on a tortoise.
Cats rest their paws on her shoulders.
What colors remain increase her charm.

Herakles has given the Centaur
a death blow. The target-headed bird
may be the Centaur's soul.

Theseus absconds with Korone,
whom Helen tries to rescue;
Herakles, pajama-clad, champions her.
He probably held a bowl in his hand.

PRE-MAGELLAN DAYS

There were storms on the sun
that disrupted radio transmission
all over the world
(fire splashing for miles)
while I was looking for
a lost shoe
in a one-room apartment.

And today, when I spent
every other hour
standing on my head,
I arrived at some belated conclusions:

Columbus was morally irresponsible;
like Galileo, he couldn't keep a secret.
Pre-Magellan days were more exciting.

ZOOM

The hefty German waitress told us
Route 9 runs into interstate 505
There is a turn off
where white birds fly from your thoughts
and the memories of your life
become the images for future dreams
She was very merry
She scratched herself and wiped the counter clean

Zoom, Zoom

MOVING

... registered on our passports

to get them through Iranian Customs

& avoid paying duty for 3 Persians

Mama Ali & Aik Bar who hired us in exchange

for food lodging cash and transportation

from Istanbul to Teheran in the middle of winter

over narrow unpaved mountain roads

3 mud-spattered Mercedes without snow tires

stuffed with plastic flowers radios crates of oranges

to get side-swiped by trucks stuck in snow

stalled on hills and edges of cliffs

Craig describing how he used to trip out

in the engine room of an Alaskan trawler

as he drove along always between the other 2 cars

to prevent us from taking off in the one we were in

because we were trusted as little as we were fed

the food in restaurants depleted

during the fast of Ramadan

although we did barge into this place one night

pointing at what we wanted in the kitchen

carcasses hanging from the rafters

a pile of orange sheep skulls in the corner

but the waiter tormenting Penny

feeling her each time he served a plate

until one of us shook him until he was smiling

like monkeys smile when they're afraid

and we had to get the hell out of there

Mama already had the cars warmed-up

and cursing the Turks apologetically offered

Penny a gum-ball of O

which she ate before we slept in a parking lot

and kept the motors running to keep us warm

then had to stop right after starting up

the next morning Penny leaning out the door

puking softly in the snow and then smiling

returning to the notebook she had

constantly reworking a sketch of a wild stallion

that she'd colored in with the blood from her first fix

Craig rolling up his swansdown sleeping bag

the best there is

Istanbul–Teheran '68

CRISIS

The other night my husband
invited his boss over for dinner.
They're in the shoe business together
so the conversation was quite lively.
Everything was going perfectly,
I'd spent a great deal of time preparing the meal,
the steaks (marinated) were on the table
and Dave, he's my husband, opened the first bottle
of beer, Piels, of course.
The cap slipped off but no one heard
that pop of vitality and flavor
we had all come to expect when using this product.
Instead, there was nothing but an unnerving,
echoing silence which permeated the room.
Dave's boss didn't miss a thing (he's that type)
and the amiable expression he had on his face
all evening suddenly became quite serious.
And it only grew worse when Dave decided to pour
the beer anyway and this flat, discolored liquid
filled a glass I'd just polished minutes ago.
Dave's boss gave him an unbearable look,
his brow was knotted like a rope,
his eyes darkened forebodingly
and I knew in my heart Dave's job
and our future were in jeopardy.

GOOD NEWS

I was at a beach I used to go to as a child,
Crab Meadow, I was down past the jetty, looking
Over the marsh grass out to the Sound where a
Herd of hippopotamuses were leaping like dolphins
Through the water; tremendous and musical,
Smiling furry hippos: I knew I was dreaming
And I knew it was the merriest dream I'd ever
Had. I was watching them from a shed and the
Window shrunk and two of the hippos climbed through
As the rest went leaping by. They stood upright
And were glad to see me, they were no bigger than
Big Beaver, they shook themselves off and I was
Glad to see them too. They had some good news,
Some great, exciting news that they couldn't wait
To tell me but the

MILEAGE

tuesday/

> Whatever happens to feel good. or peculiarly bad.
> a formless cluster, something obtained
> by its own momentum: a star, or perhaps
> a sexual experience, a piece of paper
> suspended in the wind.

monday/

> I want to start something I can't finish;
> wander around covering up my tracks
> so it looks like I'm always beginning.
> Achievement piles up like garbage.
>
> Maybe I'll do something juvenile and terrible,
> like destroy a piano with an axe.
>
> pages torn from a spiral notebook.

saturday/

> Two cats we own: a white one called Moby
> and another whose name hasn't been replaced
> since Martha realized Fellatio wasn't
> a character from Hamlet.

saturday, twice/
     I'll be constructive!

     rent a dozen accordion players
     and get them lost in a blizzard.

     pages torn from a spiral

one day/
     On the Good Ship Catatonia
       to the Isle of Catatonia . . .
    last night—
         brandy and moonlight,
   this afternoon
       I grew a pimple

sunday/
     I decrease

monday/

tuesday/
     Rules . . . inserting the bars in your own cage.

       pages torn from a spiral
       and dropping from my hand like a leaf

thursday/
> We held hands and strolled out under the stars,
> with a casual authority, I pointed out
> various constellations:
>> Orion
> the Dippers

>>> Labia Majoris

>> Labia Minoris   Solar Plexus

the next day/
> Remember lying in the woods
>> on a pile of mulch
> bark peeling off a log
>>> revealing wormlife

>> . . . ridicules

> vermiculate scrawl, an arabesque

> torn from a spiral . . . falling like a leaf

saturday/
>> I'm getting tired
>>> but I'll be gracious:
>> Geronimo died of natural causes in 1909.
>> The State of Vermont, to deter buggery,
>> outlawed the wearing of hip-boots
>> in any pasture at night.

>> A cheetah can outrun a greyhound.

saturday, twice/
An ending is dawning on me

a grimace has replaced the Cowboy's
charming smirk.
Fatally wounded, his legs buckle
and he falls to the ground,
bites the dust,
both revolvers still blazing

FLUX

Years ago, "before your time,"
we didn't have the so-called benefits
of electronic advances.
Midgets in red vests and knickers
would strut
through luxuriant high-ceilinged parlors
   holding a message on a silver plate
and call in a loud voice:
                Paging Crazy Raymond!
                Paging Crazy Raymond!

These days, crowds race randomly
through the concourses of Grand Central Station
with the same fervid mayhem
of the red and white corpuscles in their veins
(a confusion whose destination
makes sense only to some "higher-up")
and the stentorian calls
from the loudspeakers:
Crazy Raymond, report to the information booth!
Crazy Raymond, report to the information booth!
never reach the ears
of those anxious commuters below.

LAMENT

The Committee for Tomorrow
brought the options for a positive future
into the public arena
and you weren't there.
This forum for social action
permitted your direct participation
in meeting tomorrow's critical challenges
and you were nowhere in sight.
The Committee gave you the opportunity
to be involved with important personages
of Government, the Arts, the Sciences,
Business and Religion
and you blew it.
The Committee invited you
to bring your ideas and share them
with others who will listen and act
and you didn't have the courtesy
to even reply.
You could have met the Experts,
heard their views and given yours
but you didn't bother.
You forfeited your chance
to benefit personally from the Committee's
5 Practical Guidelines on how to
(1) Eliminate the adversary mode
of Conflict Resolution
(2) Unify participants and expel
myopic Disciplinary Viewpoints

(3) Replace these Viewpoints
With a holistic Approach
(4) Actively communicate Essential Information
and (5) Engage all participants
in the Decision Making Process.
Now what will you do,
where will you be
when everyone else has gone ahead,
when there's nothing left here
one morning but an occasional cloud
sliding down the river
and the crane swinging its shovel
over to the pile of gravel for the last time?
What'll happen to you
after the last dump truck pulls into position,
the last of the gravel is scooped up
and the shovel swings back
with the final load?
After the last burst of dust,
after the jaws open
and the gravel drops into the back of the truck,
you'll just be standing there
in the yellow sky
watching the safety rules being observed
for the last time,
watching the shovel swing over your head
and drop into the river,
see it raised and swung back
with water spilling from its clenched teeth
and hear the final splash
as it washes down the load.
You'll be standing there

looking back and forth
between your first and last names
while the last signals are exchanged,
the last load delivered
and dumped and paved over
with the last mix of cement,
wishing you had the foresight to have been here
when the Committee for Tomorrow
cut the ribbon and opened
the first mile of the New Highway.

CROATOAN

The drought left the earth in pieces;
parched, brittle ground curving out of view.

The shepherds were brought back by a blindman,
following his metronomic cane like penguins.
Anxiety crawled off our faces
replaced by that look what's-her-name has
when Clark Gable manages to bail out
                                in time.

All Christendom cheered. The ladies
                        waved their panties.

Loaves of Silence.

We relaxed under invisible currents,
admiring the width of the clear sky
and ascribed the appearance of a cloud
to the formation of a truly beautiful idea.

CIRCADIAN

Her clothes slid off with the ease
that makes smoke
rise and we waded in gradually, two thoughts
entering a consciousness dove
and came up shining, laughing as the water
laughed against her belly.
We felt the waves move through us
and our hips began to carry the motion.
It would have been the same
with our eyes closed: the black water
shedding light, a trail of phosphorous
to pour over ourselves
as we drifted ashore, sight reflected in sound,
synchronous crickets and stars.

from THE BOOK OF HOPE

The Sea: Instructions for abandoning ship.

Protect yourself by holding one arm over your head so your bicep is against one ear and your hand cups the other. Pinch your nose with your free hand and jump, legs straight and heels touching. If the water is covered with burning oil, emerge swinging arms in a wild, rotating manner. Continue splashing and kicking until help arrives. If the ocean is infested with blood-crazed sharks, don't panic. You are in no danger while the fins are above the surface. Once the fins are no longer visible is a sign that the sharks have turned on their bellies for the attack. This is the time for direct action. Take a deep breath and completely submerge your body. A shark's most sensitive spot is its nose. Punch the sharks in the nose until they disperse. To avoid chafing on the sharks' uncommonly rough skin, wear gloves.

The Sky.

A parachute that fails to open is an unfortunate but not altogether hopeless mishap. The quick-witted trainee will begin an immediate study of the approaching terrain. Having done his homework, he'll recall that his body can be maneuvered in certain ways to determine the speed and direction of his descent. He should aim for safe spots that will accommodate his landing. White areas denote snow; darker areas, soft, moist ground. Choice of trees should be limited to pines and willows. Remember, mud breaks your fall better than water.

The Wilderness.

When attacked by an enraged bear, anything goes. Amateurs should not have qualms about fighting dirty. But don't waste precious moments on useless tactics; the beast will not be deterred by a kick to the groin. One should make a torch, post-haste, and wave it vigorously in the bear's eyes. If one chooses to run instead, keep in mind that this beast is not adept at running downhill.

The best thing to do when bitten by a poisonous snake is just relax; sit in the shade and relax. Excitement will only speed the poisoned blood to your vital organs. The Green Mamba's bite is fatal in 3 seconds. If bitten by the Green Mamba, relax as quickly as possible.

SLOW POEM

all the boats at their moorings
     swallows darting between the spiles
we finished the coffee
        tossed the ropes onto the dock
  and sputtered around the jetty
hoping the sun would burn off the scud

saw a trawler and
     where the terns were diving
threw the lures over the stern
  trolled for Blues at three knots

       poles in the locks
        the lines slack
slight curl of the wake tracing
an hour around our expectations
        one black duck
      fast and low over the water

the overcast thick   heavier
   reeled in the lines
       and headed back to the slip
put the poles away
   and hosed down the deck
waited about three months and wrote this

Sag Harbor, June '70

CALENDAR

*with selections from
the verse of Edgard deBris
especially translated and adapted
for each month of the year*

On Fame

			JANUARY			
S	M	T	W	T	F	S
	1	2	3	4	5	6
7	8	9	10	11	12	13
14	15	16	17	18	19	20
21	22	23	24	25	26	27
28	29	30	31			

Thelonius the carpenter could hammer a nail
through a window without breaking the glass.
But now dogs spend the day in his yard
licking clamshells. And whatever became of
his slovenly offspring?

On Words

			FEBRUARY			
				1	2	3
4	5	6	7	8	9	10
11	12	13	14	15	16	17
18	19	20	21	22	23	24
25	26	27	28			

Debacle! Aye, in this very word
there is a fragrance of fatality and purity:
a beach with dead angels washed ashore,
stacked like broken ice before a land
of stolid windmills. No wonder this is
the favorite word of both shepherd and sultan.

On Cruelty

			MARCH			
				1	2	3
4	5	6	7	8	9	10
11	12	13	14	15	16	17
18	19	20	21	22	23	24
25	26	27	28	29	30	31

In Iberia, the people gather wood for fuel
and carry it home on burros.
If a burro, as is its wont, refuses to move
a fire is made under its belly.
Hence, wood is scarce in Iberia, nights
are cold and the Iberians wish for
the boundless fulfillment
of an empty bottle dropped into the sea.

On Lust

Successful, hardworking, bilingual
alchemist, 45, seeks woman of similar
background and educational experience,
compatible age desirous, must enjoy
badminton and taxonomy, strong possibility
to explore life together permanently.

APRIL						
1	2	3	4	5	6	7
8	9	10	11	12	13	14
15	16	17	18	19	20	21
22	23	24	25	26	27	28
29	30					

On Longing

Where won't you be
when I'm alone . . .

the leaf-shaped spaces between the leaves

MAY						
		1	2	3	4	5
6	7	8	9	10	11	12
13	14	15	16	17	18	19
20	21	22	23	24	25	26
27	28	29	30	31		

On Wisdom

Excreto ergo sum
or:
The young man climbed the mountain
and exclaimed: I am a thousand feet high!
When the old man reached the summit,
he observed: the mountain is five feet higher

JUNE						
					1	2
3	4	5	6	7	8	9
10	11	12	13	14	15	16
17	18	19	20	21	22	23
24	25	26	27	28	29	30

On Fear

The Champions of Darkness speed by
in their coaches, dropping cigar stubs
that spin and sparkle in the night
like harmless fuses.
There is nothing to fear but fear itself.

On Commerce

The sea has been kind to the stalwart Phoenicians.
Heading upriver, their old barks
wear white moustaches under their prows.
But after a stay in Phoenician harbors,
where the bridges and riggings are bedecked
with lanterns hanging in the night
like pearls on the neck of a Nubian maid,
the resurgent barks are fit
to mightily plow the seas once again.

On Beauty

Effendi, I have met one of the fabled
Leaf People of the Jos Plateau.
All she was wearing, Effendi, were a few
baobab leaves stuffed between her legs
and a silver coin implanted in her lower lip
which protruded exceedingly.
And when she talked, Effendi, I was mesmerized
by the raindrops that slid off the trees
above her and bounced off this coin in her lip:
an intricate marvel of punctuation
that I fear is beyond our resources.

On Crusades

In every matchbook I open, Effendi,
all I see are the faceless, silent regiments,
the helmeted troops plucked
out of rank one by one.

OCTOBER

		1	2	3	4	5	6
7	8	9	10	11	12	13
14	15	16	17	18	19	20
21	22	23	24	25	26	27
28	29	30	31

On Memory

NOVEMBER

					1	2	3
4	5	6	7	8	9	10
11	12	13	14	15	16	17
18	19	20	21	22	23	24
25	26	27	28	29	30

On Propriety

Face pressed against the window,
cold glass keeping me awake.
Owls perched on my elbows,
dead jokes stuffed in their cheeks
turning into a mouthful of smoke.
Darkness settled at the bottom of the night,
in the pines, below a leopard's
starry sense of infinity.
Rims of the brass horns barely visible out there.
Why do the musicians always tip their hats
before sinking into the river?

DECEMBER

						1
2	3	4	5	6	7	8
9	10	11	12	13	14	15
16	17	18	19	20	21	22
23	24	25	26	27	28	29
30	31

PROLOGUE

A seasonal stir; the man behind the counter
   wears a short-sleeve shirt,
customers order Coke instead of coffee,
   a few animals have collided
with cars and lay upside down on the pavement.

At least a month ago, there were still stretches
   of snow on the mountains;
winter had gone ahead of its shadows, but then
   some of the white days
returned in pieces, with unresolved thoughts
   that had been discarded and
the ice that flowed back down river from the north.

And the evenings that broadened in the wake
   of the afternoons
are now reduced by more immediate things:
   the mountains have risen
with the blossoming trees and the slopes enclose
   the road with a full
yet inaccessible green. Umbrellas sprout
   instantly in the rain
and on sunny days a woman with chubby arms
   sprouts from each window;
wasps walk along the faded sills, staggering
   at first under the weightless

feeling of a heavy load having been removed,
a confusing lightness
their imagination allows to fall upward for an
awkward but opportune conclusion.

IMPORTANT REPERCUSSIONS

Well, it's over now.
I'm exhausted but gratified.
I'd like to thank you for all your support.
I'm sure you know what I mean
when I say that.
You've been a great help.
My heartfelt regards and appreciation.
Together (and this isn't the first time
I've said so) I thought we were
a Renaissance ideal made manifest:
a multitude in unity.
I think it worked.
More than that, it's been an unqualified success.
Nobody, least of all, myself, knew
what to expect at first.
But now we do know and this alone
has touched us all.
Those of you who were with me from the beginning
remember the night we first talked about it
and the storm that we greeted
as a propitious accompaniment to our conversation:
thunder shaking the roof and the aluminum drains,
lights flickering on and off like black lightning.
1 thousand 2 thousand 3 thousand, we counted
aloud the seconds between the lightning
and thunder, the white cat leaping crazily
out of the tall grass
each time the lightning flared,

leaping against the picture window,
sliding down in a wet smear
as we toasted the success of our new venture
and, as in any undertaking of epic proportions,
invited the gods to join us.

By the next morning, only an undaunted few
were still committed.
Brass doorknobs in the gray day,
the supplicatory posture of leaves
beneath the trees from which they fell;
azaleas and dogwoods surrounded by the petals
the rain had shaken off them during the night.
I'm sure you remember having found me
just where I'd been when you retired for the evening:
in the hammock slung with so many cobwebs
between the cherry trees,
the sky suffused with a lambent pessimism
that hadn't evaded me, my work
or the wine that remained in my glass.
The night before
I had been a custodian in the arsenal of silence
but now I was the supervisor:
the starkness of those trees, the damp bark,
scaffolds upon which the harbingers
of our great idea entertained us,
busily transforming the invisible
into the visible and back again.
Two skies dueling for the day, gray and white,
as we refilled our glasses and made our plans.
You recall those early attempts,
troublesome but promising, a false

but heartening sense of accomplishment
as the odometer turning from 9,999
registered the first 10,000 miles.
And the unforeseen problems when we did succeed:
the increasing scope of our visions
inhibited the simplest acts,
an excessive tolerance and comprehension
that enfeebled us with passivity;
emptiness having no shore in our minds.
Many days I'm sure you'll never
forget; no work done, malignant stillness,
radios foolishly left on with the hope
that the sound of the music
would have some effect on the air we breathed;
observations snuffed, vexations,
the ineffable thoughts that hovered
near us and then fled
at the approach of a description.
And still we persevered,
kept climbing into the scandent clouds
though knowing, when we turned
and looked back, that language had failed us:
just the rocky slope behind us,
only a suffix or a prefix
protruding from a stump or boulder,
an –ism, or a –tion scurrying for cover.
And yet we persevered,
restoring each other's confidence
when it failed, slapping each other
on the back, forestalling that wish
to float out to the morning sea on a bare mattress.
Taste of a stale infinitude,

staring through the hours, the vicissitudes,
a blanket of pins, a blanket of birds.
I couldn't have done it without you,
lying down at dusk, casting the shadows adrift,
the slow blur of a moment ago; reminding
ourselves to blink once in a while,
blink with diurnal vastness.
None of us would be here now
if it weren't for the mutual encouragement
that sustained us through the most hazardous times.
I'm sure I speak for all of you
when I say that. We'll never forget
some of the places we visited, wondering
what we were doing there,
talking to the fisherman
as they reeled in their question marks
from the other side of the rain
or waking up only to see the swans glide away
with our best thoughts tucked under their wings.
I don't have to remind you of these things again,
although there are few besides us
who can share stories such as these.
But we did it
and this should make us proud.
Maybe no one knows about it but us
but 100,000 tons of stardust fall on the earth
every day and how many people know that?
What we did is significant
and may well prove to be a milestone,
a hallmark of human aspirations.
Yes, it might someday be of interest
to an archeologist digging around

this, our present civilization,
inspecting the shards of a vociferous but deaf people
and compare them to trees
smothered in their own fallen leaves
while looking on what we have done
as an achievement of major proportions.

TUNE

Purple angels in the wake of the sun
asking me what time it was

I told them not to worry
It was anybody's guess.
As soon as it was dark,
I burned their nests.

SQUALK

About 880 A.D.
    in Andalusia
        Abdul Abbas Kasim Ibn Firnas

built
    a flying machine

... all that sky, Effendi, and no wings ...

SERENADE

I want to climb over your hedge tonight
walk barefoot across your lawn
and shake
the fruit out of your tree

AERIAL

for Ann

Think of all the Logicians,
    the righteous afternoons we spend
watching their footprints evaporate around us
    and the extinct holidays that swirl
over our heads at night like galaxies

In the morning, moths
    careening into the sun. No tiresome
predictability but progressions and robins
on the lawn that evolved into the number 5

Summer fumes, winter crust on the sand,
    sand made to walk on with glass bodies
while the disheveled spirits of nuns
    hurtle lyrically by us
and flocks of crows soar over the shoulders
    of marble statues

homage to Saturn
           white eyes
            tilted seaward

      . . . eyes that were a wand
and rays of sunlight that guide us
to a nest of stones, mussels
    gaping and gray in the mudbanks
and the empty ones washed ashore

with the shells still connected
             so they die and open
      pearly white, blue and black, open

          like the wings of a
                    butterfly
                      blue jay
                      mallard
                    gazelle
                      corsair

STUFFED OWL

Nudged by pink-nosed clouds to sleepwalk
   through lunchtime crowds,
         Big Mama's rousing laughter,
apple blossoms sprinkled on hospital workers
    The odor of new basketballs
and car interiors
         Check the oil, please
Yes, it's really spring
the first drops of sweat running down my ribs.
This is the city of Los Angeles
  I work here
    I carry a badge

SOLO

Suggested reading time: 4'

In the name of Allah, the compassionate, the merciful;
a brief reference to corruption in desert places; how
an Englishman discouraged customs officials and
why the word noon contains a double o . . .

The first time I woke up
the water was tickling my neck.
A drowsy web of sunlight cast over the blue pool,
dead crickets floating under my chin.
The second time I woke up
I was still on the bus,
miles to go before the border,
massive old Buick engine, jostling corrugated road
the bus about to split its riveted seams;
dust covering the windows,
rising like steam through the floorboards.

Almost every passenger a smuggler.
Delayed in the last village by constables
who demanded an exorbitant bribe.
Nothing to eat there but cold rice, strips of gritty bread
to munch on with the Chitral hash supplied by
this Englishman: neatly cut hair, impeccably attired
amidst the flies and heat and, in his knapsack,
hiding all the kilos, a pile of feculent underwear
which has so far discouraged customs officials.

The bus lurching in the ruts.
Pretty, cheerful harlots in the rear seats
howling with each bounce; parrots, parakeets in cages,
goats, sheep shitting, lunging over each other,
chickens squabbling; the Persians in turbans wrapped
around their brows like taffy, the Pakistanis
in glossy caricole caps, all their heads synchronized,
turning lethargically to spew mouthfuls of nutshells
into the narrow aisle.
Lurching, peristaltic, anaconda motions
relieved when, just before the border, the bus stops,
spills over like a cornucopia in the middle of nowhere.
Everyone out to pray.

Pissing my initials in the sand,
the sky white, glaring, prolonged noon,
Moslems standing, kneeling, crouching
in the bright sand, murmuring, then louder
in black vaporous robes and veils,
women wailing in the double sun,
moving in and out of postures,
shadows searching for a shape;
afloat in this silence again,
curious where the white night ends,
rising like a kite,
shadow in a pool beneath my feet.

Coming attractions.
A day turns to an extra blank page on the calendar,
the bus bathed in the light of an absent future,
tarpaulin being pulled off the roof,
luggage and bicycles thrown down from the rack.

No one getting back on
but off they go, to bypass the border station,
tottering on overloaded bikes,
smugglers heading for the purple mountains
where the soldiers hunt for them in planes.

Pakistan–Iran '68

FEVER AND CHILLS

I am having my doubts about this expedition

Zeppelins follow me around in my sleep
like affectionate pets
The years slip by in convoys
How can I tell
if the whales beneath them are sorrowful or not
When I wake up I wonder
where they could have gone in such a small arena
My definitions of morning have had to be enlarged

And fine mornings they are, too
And delicate
The mushrooms crumble
at the approach of a worrisome thought
Even calm efforts
have set off extravagant catastrophes
How can I reveal something without destroying it
The sides of cliffs are full of exiled comedians
and their beards of ice are melting in the sun
(I wave to them from my private train)

The continuing city I've discovered
has presented me with trophies and kind regards
spider webs shimmering in the breeze
the doors the cats stare at
buildings divided by thoughts
white nocturnes

a black girl juggling lemons
Soon it will pass me by
I contacted Malaria and this is what she said
Meanwhile, provisions exist in ample amounts
You might not recognize me when I come home
                Scratch my ass
. . . this phrase is now my signature

SOUTH OF SOKOTO

Nigeria, '67
for Peter Schjeldahl

I.

A bat flew into the room and knocked itself
from wall to wall.
We ducked and swung, protecting our eyes
and the lantern
            but Yusufu got it, smacked
it to the ground and played with it for a while.

Momo, convinced Americans didn't speak English,
interrupted himself occasionally to make sure
I understood the words he was using:

            You know "Shame" Mister Fol?
            You know "Phlegmatic" Mister Fol?

How about a cup of coffee, I offered,
            or do ya wanna mail a letta?

Ibrahim poured himself another cup and warned:
            You drink coffee too much,
        make you want to crack women plenty, crack
                women plenty!

Bala snickered, showing his filed teeth.

II.

Riverbed

    wide and dry like the day

white river

    swirling through the fields

and women walking home in single file
black swans over bleached sand.

A baby asleep, carried on his mother's back

flies huddled on his crusty eyelids,
his turgid navel the size of a lightbulb.

Donkeys squinting in the sun

    a dull axe chopping wood
a sledge cracking stone

    Another woman floats by like a sound

White birds walking on straw
   step between the legs of grazing cattle

a silver snake sliding into a rivulet

Sundown   the bare limbs liquefy   shimmer

red monkeys loping along a hilltop

III.

Funtua Town. The restaurant crowded, everyone
        squatting frog-like or leaning
against the cane-stalk walls,
        watches each spoonful
of rice, diced meat, yams go into my mouth.

That night the waitress—
her hair tightly knit and knotted into braids,
                        upright, antennae;
her skin lighter where her breasts swelled,
        they seemed to glow inside.

"Sha" was the Hausa verb for both
water and smoking: someone asks for fire
    instead of a match,
someone "drinks" the smoke.

Her name had a "sha" in it, I think.
Her brother introduced himself as The Chairman.
He sold India Hemp by the cinema
        and called it Bubbly-Bubbly.
It's carbonated, he attested.

She gave me a necklace with medicine
and prayers sealed in four leather pouches
and told me what each would do;

while explaining she poked my heart,
she stroked my hands, she patted my crotch,
she kissed my eyes;

one was to keep me healthy, she said,
one to keep me free, one was for good
loving, the other would keep me sane.

We leafed through her foto collection together
    pages filled with circus freaks
from the, uh, four corners of the globe.
She had loved the politician, Balewa, and his
portrait was printed on the robes she wore.
"When the Ibo killed him," she said, "the ladies,
they cry in the streets that night."

The flame's shadow wobbled under the low candle,
then quickened, rolling softly with her hips.
        You palaver man, she said,
            me palavar lady . . .

Drove home drunk, verily drunk
wearing the wind for a great cape,
the scooter vibrating wildly,
the road bumpy as a blindman's shins.

Stars clear and near,
bugs twirling in the headlight beam.
And then saw the fields burning,
set afire by farmers

and pulled out of the ruts   rode back and forth
through the high and lovely flames
windy flag-flapping sound
dragon laughter

scarlet and smokeless
turn the night upside down

Slept near there
on back of the scooter

woke up, a white cow examining my face
big bulging eyes

fat cows in the burned fields

APPROACHING URANUS

Will everyone have a front row seat
Do our eyes appear as headlights
Does the glow increase while we think
Explain these nipples on my chest
Where was the Land of Cockaigne
What about the face of Charlemagne
Why warts
Did someone discover the wheel by stepping
   on his fingers at the brink of a hill
Can you appreciate the modulations of a vicious belch
Where are the plays of Menander
Does the Loch Ness Monster ring a bell
Do impure souls lend color to the flames
Do you find these myths entertaining
Or superfluous
Am I a Calvinist
Whither Martin Bormann
Has someone already asked you these questions
Have I already asked you these questions
How will I know you're not lying
How will you know you're not lying
Is perfection comforting
What if it isn't

SITE

Gulping down a bottle of wine
four red faces with yellow teeth
huddled against the cold

The day ended early
a faint three-thirty sun
(one you can look at
without squinting)

Letters from a sky-writer
now illegible
fading into cirrus clouds

The year peeled away
to Winter's blank canvas
and a bird flying south
using only one wing

APOCALYPTIC

A man will appear bearing this sign
On a matchbook cover:
An Eagle flying atop the letter I
And encircled by a dark ring.
He will be an agent
Of the Independent Insurance Company.
Invite him into your home.
Feed him.
Bid him well.
He will visit many.
He will visit those who have nailed
The Bald Eagle above their door,
He will visit those who have placed
The duck on their lawns;
He will appear to every sect:
Those of you with the Flamingo
Before your home,
Those whose names are inscribed in Brass
And those whose names are hung from Lamps:
He will visit those who have put the statue
Of the Blue Lady in their gardens,
He will talk with you,
He will hold an umbrella
Over your Auto, your House, your Life.
He will comfort you and allay your Fears.

LOOSE ENDS

Between the prairie and the ocean a woman snores.
    She dreams of a seed a bird
can carry but the wind can't blow away.
    Students practice subtraction
on local hilltops. A shift in planetary gears
    and the sky would fall, they're
told, and lie down more dented and crumpled
    than a field of snow. Sirens
at the firehouse would not churn every noon
    and throughout the United States
a chorus of dogs wouldn't reply to what they
believed was the song of a Celestial Bitch . . .

Maybe the same woman awakes smelling like glass.
    A light snowfall always ends
with a gentle dance of confusion, and for a moment
    or two, things are out of focus.
Once they resume their normal positions, the air
    is clear. And she lights a cigarette.
Her age is 8 o'clock. The smoke forms a bouquet.
    An ash drops, shattering the ashtray.

ON THE SURFACE

aroma— elevated forms of wool-bearing animals
cinema— an asian girl with an african name
torpor— the fate of mastodons
bandito— a minor bandage
scoundrel— a french goblet for special occasions
Monotony— when capitalized, an extinct south-sea god
plenitude— where albatross prefer to land
anglo-saxon— a frenetic dance of the twenties
endow— to retrieve an ear
antiquity— a hollow man swallowing tears
sponsor— a musical insecticide
index— the navel's reply
Zavatsky— the conductor addresses the woodwinds
agog— someone whose feet never stopped growing
oregon— frozen ink
tin— an epicine curse
adventist— any famous person with tooth decay
bizarre— the mole, reconsidered
Betty— at 3 o'clock high, unfriendly aircraft
metaphor— I use them. They keep me regular.
niggardly— an adverb
vehemence— paper butchers used for wrapping veal
overture— not a Haitian revolutionary

AIRFIELDS

1.

A cure for a constricted soul
membership in the supernal claque

and a slow escalator for the ride back up
past benign planets and floating cats.

Then wings are formed by sheer aspiration.
The arena is a state of being
supplied by an abandoned winter beach
and the performing colors are from Chinese Opera:
Red and Black represent virtues,
Gold faces for gods, Green for spirits;
a delight in what survives,
motion and illumination.

2.

For meager but compulsory reasons
there were daily ascents:
living in a six-flight walk-up,
pieces of conversation overheard at each landing
and odors of different meals.
Six *flights* of stairs,
a term of exacerbating irony;
prayers for Sisyphus. The last

the slowest turn of the spiral,
but if detached from the drudgery
an extra flight was attained
and the door opened to the sky
and a great Silver hound chasing its tail.

3.

. . . the match is tilted downward
so the budding flame may rise)

All day the moon has been in the cat's eyes
waxing, waning according to the available light

and yesterday, before and after the rain
a succession of hills, Green fading to Gray,
to what is familiar enough to be recognized
without the assurance of it being
either a remembrance or a reckoning.
Now the water is flowing the other way,
textures varying from sharkskin to glass.
Somebody's child in Red sneakers

4.

Or, in the brightness of these Grecian hills
the day burning in its own reflection,
gnarled and twisted Olive trees
indicate a difficult history of martyrdom.
Explorers return with humility.

The last one burned his maps and said:
I owe it all to centrifugal force.
Each one speaks of a darkness that had been a star
and of the light that continues to flow from there,
a confounding whiteness, either ultimately
full or blank, moved by inherent contradictions
and having the stillness of a propeller's blur.

SCROUNGE

Delhi '68

Motorcycles modified with canopied carts,
bearded driver circling the rotaries,
turbaned Sikhs with silver bracelets.

Buildings along Chandni Chowk leaning together,
balconies sagging, cows stalling traffic,
upsetting shops and spilling sacks of grain;
one defecates in the street,
a girl runs out,
the crap scooped up, patted into a pie
and smacked onto a wall to dry for fuel,
her handprint neatly impressed on it;
bringing to mind: a stop sign
or an Islamic emblem for good luck.

A lunch of curry, eggs, yogurt, tea
licorice seeds and out into the sun.

Holymen with staffs and bowls, weak and spindly
unlike that one in Benares . . . ebullient, talking
to a crowd, oily black hair pulled back in a knot,
as naked as he was big,
balls tucked in under the immensity of his belly
      smiling
           smiling

The Moroccan moping in the hotel room again
complaining he keeps getting shoved out of line
because his skin is dark
and he's mistaken for an untouchable;
and the others talking; laughing
about being the anomaly, the poor white man.

   So much depends
     on a regimental tie
       a three-piece suit

      and the right shoes
    shining
        under tweed cuffs

At least the children don't sneer at you

but in Benares
you can stay on houseboats
near the ghats on the Ganges . . .
And the chellum passed around
cinders fall onto the greasy quilt
eyes sliding across the room
to fingers tapping on a Tabla

Soak up vagaries like a sponge,
beautiful women dismiss themselves
and disappear into misty pools.

2nd Class waiting room
tessellated with sleeping Indians one night,
contrapuntal snorts and snores
and not any warmer than it is on the street.
　　Shake off this daylong dejection
　　like a dog in out of the rain
and arrange six chairs into a cot,
pull some clothes out of the knapsack;
it feels odd getting dressed to go to bed,
teeth chattering so hard I thought they'd break
and then lie down
almost melting to sleep:
bad news and bothersome thoughts drifting away
with a riled, murky stream
　　　　　　　resuming a clarity that—
but a guard raps on the chair
demanding a ticket and there's nothing
to do except argue, snarl at each other
in our respective languages
until everyone else complains about the commotion
and then it's a matter of obstinacy:
a staring contest,
but he blinked first and lost.

A cold body curls into itself
　　a wet leaf in a flame . . .

And then what should have been a dream,

change without effect
          . . . following my own tracks through the snow,
      the fresh snow

Complicated vacancies and inevitably
experiences that lacked a moral emphasis
swarm back with fury, with infinite consequence;
banshees flying down through abandoned monuments,
demonic, perverse images of a ruined city.

Instances like that and the questions
which prey on them; a pause inquiring
what endures, what recurs bringing peace.

Or, no matter where, to always have been walking
    on that beach, year upon year;
the month of the teetering solstice
and the clouds have woven a blank together,
cerement upon cerement
dulling the sun to the brightest moon

        . . . lost in the flood
          and then the empty, lusterless light.

A new kind of blindness,
left with my vision but nothing to see,
        dust of a cartoon heaven
        silt of Icarian angels
        falling all over me

Racket of passengers packing their bedrolls,
get up lower than the night before:
it's still dark and this is the way out
through the 3rd Class waiting room,
stepping over bodies, untouchables, half-naked,
sprawled all across the floor, contorted faces
moaning in sleep, mottled brown skin, heads
leaning on thin biceps, misshapen pile
collapsed, fallen from the Sistine ceiling.

Out the doors into a blast of wind
paring but whetting a heart now hunched
in its cage of bones;
and a sudden tranquility:
        lanterns flare in the tea shacks;
simplicity of a fire on a chilly morning,
                coals white as frost.
A few people emerge: knobby, skinny men
wrapped in worn sheets, appearing then
as they do now, as images coaxed into the mind
. . . and encircle the flameless smoke.

No rest in sleep: tired bones
that beat themselves to stillness
and sights that remained in closed eyes
that only now open
        to a sapphire sky
and one brilliant star
above a rim of light that's rising in a dome

One diamond cross above the dawn
and the soft light spreading slowly,
so near,
    until it is felt
        reluming from within;
and grow with it, with a gratitude and relief
ineffable as the opposing night was long.
          Remember past strivings,
            remember
on the verge of jubilation
    Remember past strivings
   remember what the darkness has
          shown
me, a confluence
  a dreamsong of Mandans on Mayday
        with filaments of the sun
tied to their chests
swaying down and around around and down
    between the thick-leaved trees,
the sonar chirping of sleeping birds
to Connaught Place, the rotary park
    to watch the night drain away.
Sitting on a bench and two mongrels come
bounding across the grass back   and forth
leaping on and over each other, crouching
pouncing, one the pursuer   now the other
yelping, licking and nipping, the chase
prolonged throughout the deserted Sunday
and finally together with eyes wide open,
tongues dangling and flanks atremble.
  The singing heard then
          and followed

to a side street (a spoke in the wheel)
to a large tent with colorful, broad stripes
peaceful chanting from within, led by an elder,
men on one side   women on the other
incense burning, bells and clear voices.
A boy approaches, lays a wreath of moist flowers
over my head
        and invites me in.

IDLE

A man struggles with his shirt
His arms are tangled
in the wrong sleeves and the sun
can't find an opening in the clouds

Low tide emptied the cove and left
the ice trapped in the reeds, paper-thin
and punctured by each step the heron takes

Children whisper to burned-out lightbulbs
that are the color of the sky and they shake
them like rattles, they dance as the water
whistles through the faucets and a man
walks down a dry street in the rain

his trousers pressed, his collar clean

TRUE ADVENTURE STANZAS

As the sun rose
our hopes daffodiled
We stripped to our shirtsleeves
to meet an onslaught of widgeon
gadwalls and more pintails and teal
    This was only the beginning
     of our search for winter's hot spot

We came up against the equivalent
of hard-flying Nebraska ringnecks
wild-flushing Wyoming chukar
and explosive Dixie bobwhites
    We then waited for Curtis Peters
     avid Florida sportsman
     to put us up in his air boat

We found a deep pool
that would take the guesswork
out of ice fishing
one that produced slabsided largemouth
acrobatic ladyfish
sleek sea trout and mangrove snappers
     I have never—repeat never—seen fatter
     or harder-fighting mangrove snappers

The sun flickered out behind me
the air chilled
a doe appeared and appeared

again through my scope as a gay ghost
She sensed danger and sprang
I swung through the blur and fired
My ice prize, my winter weekend was over
Lady Luck had failed me but (continued on pg. 245)

TYRANNOSAURUS BRONX

for Allen Appel

All the elevated lakes are frozen
into the flat tar roofs of factories and schools
Air vents and chimney stacks
have been appointed plants by a metallic sun
The custodians swing their broad mops
down the vacant halls of the day's interior

The past recedes at the same rate
as the future and again leaves me high and dry
on a winter plateau that was formerly the Bronx

I relax with my head propped in my arms
watching the drowned choir that was once my toes
Their erased faces stand in unison
at the end of the bed as the Bronx begins
to revolve around a stationary record
like smoke over a doused fire

One bulldozer mounts another in an empty lot
Subway cars crawling on the trestle unfold into moths
My toes recite
            The Gray Credo

   We believe the prehistoric imagination
was immense and tender and gray
   We believe dinosaurs were smothered by
the stale purity of their imaginations

We believe there was once a color like
gray but it wasn't very serious and escaped
into the wind

We believe gray has come home to roost
over the abandoned sleep of the Bronx

AQUEDUCT RATINGS
& GULFSTREAM RESULTS

Evening Bag
Indian Joy
Colossal Dream
Dizzy Sag

Tootsie Viking
Red Ice
Lum Puckeroo
Penrage Pilgrim
Suncrowns Kid
Moaning-the-blues

Saucy Wings
Flaming Fox
King Imp
Pill Runner
Marcumba War
Conjurer

Miss Wardance
Tudor Rascal
Top Trojan
Flowing Speed
Somersault
Luminous Lagging

John The Prophet
Moon Raker
Ranger Chimes
Needles Delight
Rusty Shawnee
Dust Commander
Costly Music
Buzz Buzz

FIASCO WINES INC.

Imitations of smoke signals on a cloudy day

———————

They found him a block away from his home
yet he didn't know where he was

And he got there under his own power

———————

Beware the March of Dimes!

———————

The wet leaf slides down the window pane
like the hand of a dismissed bank teller
letting go of his dreams, his girl, his new car

———————

Moments of intense shame and regret
return in low-flying aircraft

———————

After the shower, each clover
contains a raindrop
and the possibility of a fine girl
sitting naked in my lap

———————

The prophet is confused but exhilarated
in a world of praise,
an oriole among black-eyed Susans.

———————

His future's been cancelled
due to excessive planning . . . or a thirsty man
arrives to discover somebody's taken a bath
in his drinking water

———————

Birches, Poplars, leap to brightness;
the wind falls,
a trout jumps from the lake.

———————

The fly twirls his moustache
and rubs his hands together as if sharpening them.
The locomotive rounds the bend,
the virgin writhes on the tracks.
A cloud of dust with a white hat
comes galloping across the purple sage
accompanied by a frantic piano.

FREE AND CLEAR

Each wave casually unfolds
    a minute over the beach,
            showing us how it's done
                  (sostenuto)
and the seconds, shaped by the gull's wings
  stroke   what's left of the daylight;
        time's script telling me
              lie down
under nightfall, under a dark snow, gentle
          not plentiful enough
it seems, until complete
and then more revealing than the day.
        You can see for years from here!
a view of the sea and city lights
      mingling with the galaxy.

Sleep   and assurance, perhaps
after bringing lesser conflicts to the shore
like some inadequate yet absolving sacrifice;
as if to say: when alone I am complete.
       But then come closer to an expanse
        that can turn to nothing in a moment
  (She filled space you didn't know was there. . . .
      caught me on my blind side)

      Feel exposed, vulnerable in this openness
      while the wind sharpens the grass
     fall further than sleep

Wake up. morning, a wasted beginning.
Back to town. crunch. crunch.
seeing: fat man, fat wife
          fishing on sunny rocks.
          statues.
          somebody else's statues.

PING PONG

Gentlemen, you are, no doubt, concerned about
    Headlights moving across steaming manholes
Thoughts of her come trailing along with petals
    Down the brook, the sniveling bitch
A haphazard interaction that serves
      An unexpected glimpse, slow, graceful
And shaped by a celerity that'll tickle your
       Certain recommendations must be proposed
When the world spins with a whisper, dearie
We'll leave these worshippers of simplicity our bones
The earth is good here, Martha, we will build a new home
    She cringed with delight
  (a recent account of geophagy)
    Don't cheer men, those poor devils are dying!
    This night, filtering through the Scotch Pines
      The Christmas neon sequestered in the mist
Lemon souls deep within the heart of the sea
     The swarm of yellow taxis purring anxiously
Beneath the red eye
    The red eye
That man running
      He's the fastest man in the world and

GREAT AMERICAN SOUP

for Mark Twain

Becky's mom confronted her in the doorway.
Where are you going, she demanded.
Becky said nothing.
You're going out with Tom, aren't you, she insisted.
Becky clenched her teeth.
I'm a big girl now, Mom, she said.
Becky's mom shuddered and stifled a sob.
Walk with the lame and you'll begin to limp,
She admonished. But a determined Becky
Was already on her way out the door.

Becky ran down the beach.
As she approached their rendezvous, defiance
Gave way to liberation. She felt great.
But then Tom wasn't there. She called for him.
He sneaked up behind her and startled her.
She squealed and they kissed.
He was already in his trunks.
Let's go, said Tom. Becky took of her dress.
Underneath, she wore an Esther Williams swimsuit.
Tom shook his head and whistled approval.
Catch me, squealed Becky, as she dashed into the surf.

Tom's hacking style was no match for Becky's
Graceful strokes. She turned to urge him on
But he was nowhere in sight.
What manner of tomfoolery was this, wondered Becky,

As she waited for his hands to grab her body.
But they never did. Just as her expectations were
Turning to deep concern, she felt the terrible pain,
She squealed and she too was gone.

In the morning, the Naval Intelligence experts
Returned Becky's clothes to her mom. Captain Kraken
Didn't want to cause her any further torment.
How could he explain to this simple woman that
The earthquake and the atomic tests had awakened
A horrendous creature from its subterranean slumber.
But Becky's mom needed no explanation.
She knew something like this would happen
When Becky started seeing the likes of Tom.

SONNET

for Ann

Another world arrives, bestowing all its favors
and courtesies in an avalanche of clouds.
No convenience has been ignored.
Solitude provides a limousine that transports me
to a wood thick with pale gray saplings.
Then, instead of tolerance and dry wine
I'm confronted with the dreariest consequences

       (If I decide not to reveal where the
       Zurbarans and El Grecos are hidden,
       the hostages in the village will be
       executed.

       The paintings, many of which engage
       dismal or exaggerated themes of penance
       and redemption, are in mountain caves,
       safely packed in crates fastened with
       metal straps. The villagers are a hard-
       working, selfish bunch of sots whom
       I've dealt with only on the most
       mundane levels.)

I try to apologize for my lack of concern
but this only makes me laugh louder.
My interrogators scoff at such ingratitude, they
answer their own questions, the clouds lose interest

and fade away and around the calmness in my mind
the rest of the day remains, bristling
with what the light and leaves have made of you.

THREE POEMS

Westinghouse

wurver

razzmatazz

THREE OR FOUR POEMS

Frequently the patient hears or feels
the bone snap. There is pain and tenderness
at the point of the break
        The patient can run his fingers
over the suspected point of fracture,
there will be more tenderness
        and he may be able
to feel an uneven place covered
with moss and a violet clover
indigenous to both disappointment and surprise;
        the kind that also grows
in the village where he lives, over
        its stone walls,
        its clusters of clapboard houses
and beneath the lines of white laundry
swimming in the breeze. Frequently
        a woman wanders into the yard
to see if the clothes are dry, touching
each sheet
in an absent-minded way, as though
        walking by a piano, she
would idly run her fingers over the keyboard.
The sod farm encircles her and the village,
        miles of perfectly level land
criss-crossed
        with irrigation pipes spurting
water in long arcs like great pairs
of wings always flying in her direction.

Men crouch under the spray,
slicing the sod out in sections, strong
and as well-knit as a rug.
        They fold a piece over
their shoulders, carry
        it to the flatbed wagons while
the sunlight slides over
the coleus and across the laundry and the lawn;
        a weakened but melodious light
out of which a plane, every so often, drops
and smashes through the sides of a church,
boards, shingles and hymnals blown into the air,
propeller bent, wings
        torn off, the chassis bursting
out the opposite wall. The pilot always
        wakes up unscathed, alights
from the wreckage and removes his goggles,
        slaps the dust and splinters off
his leather jacket and salutes the sky.

SAGA

1.

Lance is the only one alive. Click. Click.
He's out of ammunition! The enemy horde
converges on the outpost for the final assault.
They toss grenades at him from every direction.
He leaps atop his bunker
and, holding his rifle by the barrel, swats
the grenades back at the foe.
As soon as it is evident that there are too many
grenades in the air for one person
to reasonably deal with, maestro smacks
the dust off his baton and the band
begins to play a medley of national anthems
that soon exceeds the battle's din.
Lance continues to swing his rifle.
A pictorial history of French and English military
uniforms is displayed along the horizon
until the evening tilts further west
and pours the colors of this day
back into the setting sun.

2.

With the grand finale still resounding in his ears,
Lance is led down a flight of steps to a small, grubby
café filled with pirates, sluts, advertisers, wantons
and curs. Ants or termites have left vine-like trails
across the thick clay walls. The lanterns are few,
the place is dark and god is sitting in a corner booth.
Lance is bewildered. All the people are wearing
different expressions on their faces and he feels
as though he's in a room full of clocks with each one
telling a different time. Lance is led over to god
who looks disconsolate but cheerful, weary but young,
and wearing a torn straw sombrero, a stiff linen
shirt, smudged and stained, and two bandoliers
criss-crossed over his chest.

     Lance quickly surmises, by the way his escorts
have introduced him, that god, except for the ability
to laugh, is a mute who communicates through a
continual game of charades and mimicry. When he
inquires as to why this is so, the reply, delivered
in a series of difficult gesticulations, is that
actions speak louder than words and, nine times
out of ten, are more effective. God pours him some
wine out of a jug but misses his glass.
The implications of this act perplex
Lance but not his companions, who quickly order
another bottle and

3.

proceed to translate god's discussion with Lance
about how just as noun, plural, predators, no
Nimrods, no hunters! just as hunters
verb, use a flashlight, a bright
white light to snare, no trap, trap an animal, a
four-legged animal with horns,
deer! and bunnies, bunny rabbits, just as hunters
use a bright white light to trap deer and rabbits
at night and fishermen persuade, coax lobsters,
crabs, crabs to the top, the surface, to be scooped
up in nets, he, me, god, once relied on such
rough, uneven, obscene, fuck you too, crude!
crude manners, methods to, ah, wrest
rescue yellow rhomboids, no, lop-sided butterflies,
no, state of being, a drunken swan? no! Souls!
Souls! he too once relied on such crude methods
to rescue souls from New Jersey, no the Netherlands,
contraction, but, now he, god, correction, capital
G, God, has, long verb, energized, developed,
formed, newer, better, more economical methods,
which, verb to be, are, all the verbs to be,
more wholesome, more relaxed,
a convenient, easy-to-use, mixture, blend of ha ha
ha ha laughter and silences, solitudes, that can be,
no, that can lead to a, adjective, study-at-home-course . . .
lead to a diploma . . . an endless deliverance . . .

4.

As Lance, regaining consciousness, floats upward
to the brightening surface, he mistakes
the scorched Christmas trees falling toward him
for the fossils of an extinct black fish
until they pass close by and he notices that
what he thought were their hearts
are actually a knot of velvet ribbon,
fireproof, and some still wearing a price tag.
It must be late January, he concludes.
Aware of being transported with the easy voyaging
he knew only as a blessing of sleep, moving
him hours in an instant, from shore to shore,
moving him somnolently like a cloud,
then swiftly, like a cloud, and then finally
leaving him in a deep repose, on a patio
ensconced in the lush gardens and pure, quiet air
of a military hospital.
At first, he is confused, but his vision sharpens
and he is able to distinguish between
the birch tree and the nurses and bandaged patients
that surround his bed. Someone is holding his hand.
His eyes ascend, passing her wrist, her arm,
her immaculate neck. He looks into her eyes.
It's his fiancée! Unbeknownst to him, she
had joined the army nursing corps and through
good fortune managed to be assigned to this hospital.
Overwhelmed, he tries to speak.
"You're so beautiful," he murmurs, "your parents

should have named you Luncheonette."

They gaze silently into each other's eyes.

Everyone in the hospital looks their way and applauds.

ALBA

The train departs, lurching, locomotive
spewing smoke and sparks into the night
like a whale having a bad dream.

Starry morning

though the station platform always looks damp.
Milkweed growing through the slots
between the planks, pods unsealed
bright and silky.

Cross the tracks,
down the gravel slope and over the fence:

White sea, straw sea

the snow that froze smooth
over the field melted
months ago but the long grass
still bent in waves

birds sleeping in the empty waves

your absence crowded with thoughts of you

MEMORIES FOR
THE ELECTRIC BEARS

Trees from which the black sky bloomed
        from which the birds fell in their sleep
    edenic steam
        Iron owls bleeding fire
            on the gelid leafmold

  Were we deaf
      or had we lost our voices?

            consummate silence
            chaos

    the night we tore our shadows from

RUMOURS TO THE EFFECT

A slack sea revives the philosophers.
With the loss of direction, deliberations begin:
    the pause is mistaken for an alarming,
alien peace, they agree the destination must have
    arrived and its permanence is what
has saturated them all with an intolerable weight.
    But they'll forget themselves as soon
as the first gusts of wind pronounce the word Vanish
    against the limp canvas, repeating it
until the sails are full and the ocean's sliding by.

Meanwhile only the _____ are content,
sharing bushels of lemons, mangos, dates and almonds;
    the socks rolled off their sore feet
and their toes wiggled freely with appreciation.
    They sit cross-legged on the teak deck,
smiling, happy once again with the anticipation that
    the still water, by lowering itself
a bit, is preparing to divulge a marvelous secret.

ENDINGS

La Jolla, California '66

hear fires dying

when the wave slips in under the haze
and spreads
          sizzling
                across the dry beach
and the next one
washes a second skin of sand off my feet.

          . . . Balboa's afternoon,
the dunes and ocean indistinguishable
                              in the mist

and what once would have been described
as the sun
transformed behind the imperceptible drift
of the sky
into a cross then a supine hand

                              pacific

and for a while
knowing that explorers must lose themselves,
nostalgia for an illusion,
a world that isn't shrinking, and the notion
that the emerald light enveloping me
was once an intimation
of the earth ending in permanent genesis.

BOREDOM

for Ron Padgett

The sun folds with a royal flush
over the factory and the night shift
drops the deck and returns to work.
The building is immense and rectangular,
made of concrete blocks painted white outside
and gray within. The windows are large
but can't be looked through because they
are on the roof, to maximize the amount
of sunlight let in and minimize the cost
of electricity. When the workmen enter
the factory, they insert their time-cards
in the time-clock and go to their lockers.
They all wear gray overalls and paper hats.
This is the compulsory attire and the hats
are the butt of an inexhaustible joke: if one
worker passes another as they push
their carts down the aisle, he'll say:
"Hey, keep your hat on!"
They stack the boxes onto their carts
after removing them from the conveyor belts
and then wheel the carts out to the trucks and
freight cars parked in the rear of the buildings.
Like most factories, this one was built
in a location that affords an easy access
to railroad lines and interstate highways.
Let me think, has anything been left out?
Oh, yes, machines have been installed that dispense

coffee, cocoa, soup and crackers to the workmen.
Every man has his own locker. I already mentioned that.
But the overalls and hats are supplied without charge
and the laundry is also free.
Most of the men prefer to wear shoes with crepe soles.
Most of them drive to work in their own cars.
The foremen wear ties.
Everyone is overweight.
Production for the fiscal year that ended in April
would have exceeded all expectations
but no one had any.
Well, that does it.
I can't think of anything more to say.
It looks very tranquil here tonight.
The windows are glowing and the crickets
are, uh, what's the word for it, chirping?
The crickets are chirping in the grass
that grows along the chain-link fence
which surrounds this place. I don't know
if I've left anything out or not.
Maybe I should add that the factory may be burning.
Yes, I guess it is, it definitely is burning.
The warehouse is ablaze, that's for sure.
The flames are rather brilliant, more red than yellow,
but at this rate it's safe to say that they'll be
bright white in no time at all.
One of the warehouses is almost totally destroyed,
its steel frame is wavering in the intense flames.
Spectators have been gathering in the last few minutes.
A lot more are expected. It's going to be a long show.
Bleachers are in the process of being erected.
A few vendors are already selling refreshments.

There goes the steel frame I mentioned a few seconds ago.
Most of the refreshments are reasonably priced.
I don't recall seeing flames this tall before.
It's a veritable maelstrom, as they say.
A lot of folks came unprepared for this; walls
collapsing, roofs crumbling. Entire families
are sitting together in the bleachers,
mothers are trying to keep track of their children
and wipe the soot off their faces.
The havoc is undiminished.
It's hell out here all right.
The heat is causing some distress
among the less stalwart in the crowd.
The smoke is blacker than the late night sky,
it's billowing over our heads
dropping cinders onto people's laps.
I can see that some of the folks are getting
a bit fidgety. This is taking longer
than one would suppose. It's almost midnight
and this inferno has shown no signs of abating.
The firemen, I might add, though exhausted by now,
have not slackened their efforts in the least.
Chief Herlighy has issued a statement: he says
due to the intense winds and lack of equipment
it'll be quite awhile before this fire ends.
The steel structures of the buildings are all
twisted like the pretzels that are being peddled
here tonight at a quarter apiece, the hoses
are leaping over the ground like spastic spaghetti
and, yes, there have been casualties: one
hook and ladder man has been undone by fatigue.
The flames are what can only be described as

spectacular. Some of the spectators are beginning
to leave. There's no chance of rain.
This fire will be burning for quite a while.
I can see a pinochle game or two in progress
and a few enterprising young couples
are playing volley ball behind the bleachers
There's no lighting problem here.
Word has reached me that the police have gone home.
The wind has stopped but the fire certainly hasn't.
A lot of us are getting disgusted with all this.
Leaking hoses have turned this place into a swamp
The remaining onlookers will have a hard time
getting away. Chief (what's his name, O'herlihy?)
Chief O'herlihy has said whatever water
is getting through the nozzles
evaporates before it reaches the flames.
He's afraid this one will just have to burn itself out.
His men are weary and bedraggled
but, he reminds us, fire fighters, no matter
how dedicated they are, can't subsist on cold coffee.
He also complained that this is the worst crowd
he's had to contend with in his 40 years as a fireman.
His men, he says, could have done a better job
if they weren't harassed by nosey spectators
but it's too late now and, as he put it,
there's no sense crying over spilt milk . . .

INDUSTRIAL SONNET

Dacron Jaymar Binaca Singlex Citgo
Kool Dep Polyester No-Nox Durolite
Tab Selectmatic By-Products Texaco
Activated Linoleum Fortrel Neolite
Anacin Sanka Purolater Rayon Zippo
No-Doz GE Doral Pyrex GM Micronite
Orion Pepsi Duz Vinyl Getty Lextro
RCA Lavoris Cassette Nylon Playtex
Acrilon PanAm Teflon Doxsee Philco
Unicard Storette Techmatic Simplex
BOAC Banlon Econocar Yuban Nabisco
Windex Fab Clorox Vaseline Memorex
Propane Magicube Ikotron Descoware
Geritol Cessna Korvettes Diamonair

FOUR POEMS

First Prize

20 dark and wonderful dreams about the ice people

Voice

Nightcloud with the moon behind her

Apparition
for Ezra Pound

Petals on a wet-back's brow

Prosody

Put the cop back on the beat

THE MASTER OF CEREMONIES

for Jim Shepperd and Edna Chung

Manhattan slides in on sea-level routines,
luminous overtones that break in a final surge of clarity
over a man who had bent down to inspect an ant.
The flattened life of Captain Runt: a maze
with an obvious exit; he traced
in the course of its rampant symmetry, the edges
of the tiles, rooms and rooftops
to the neatly arranged crofts outside the city;
the television antennae blended with the withered trees
and people walked with their nose against the wall.
Morning drew him magnetically out of sleep
up to a crow's view of school buses rotting in the sun.
He began by watching the skyline light up
in the dark, room by room below the evanescent stars
as he imagined entire structures enlivened
by the feeling of all the faucets turned on
and the water pouring freely through the pipes.
At noon, he would find himself looking for the center
of a shallow pond, one he could shove
an empty car into and let it sit there
with the doors and trunk and hood open
and the windows rolled down. He had nothing to explain,
the days fit the corners and each one
extended the pattern of the maze.
He was the first to observe that roaches ride scooters.
While on evening drives, the silent nudes
on outdoor movie screens put him in the midst

of square dreams afloat in a pervasive and transparent
mind, and old people scratching themselves
behind distant windows would awaken the thought
that his existence was an unconfirmable secret.
He would itch and his house would drop another shingle.
It is the only one around whose doors
are always open to the snow. It's not old but it's ransacked
and deserted, filled with everything
he didn't know and carpeted with broken glass
that shimmers like Lee's farewell to his troops.
The house burned once and with the usual irony
only the chimneys remained. Since it was rebuilt
the forsythias bloom with a wild brightness against
its sides and stones drop from the foundation
with the suspicion that they had grown loose,
cracked the mortar and toppled back onto the ground.
It was all here.
He called it The House of Musical Traditions.
Everything breakable had been broken.
People would flock to it
from carnivals that didn't survive a storm,
bringing those who fled to their cars
with pockets full of change,
the stuffed bears with plastic eyes
that were taken off the shelves
and raindrops that didn't even break in the dust.
A kiwi and a chicken would come out to greet them,
to sit on the warped steps
together and watch the sunlight on the river
recite the Emancipation Proclamation backwards.
Growing smaller and smaller with every breath,
they wanted nothing more than to know

how to contend with the inexplicable;
they wanted nothing less than to have
anything explained to them.
So he devised miraculous failures, telling them
of the time he was conducting his orchestra
and the symphony that got tangled in his baton,
of the deflated crescendos and the musicians
who stood there squinting, trying to
recognize themselves as the dwarfs they'd become.
That was when all the corners
were turned and the birds jumped about on the phone
lines like notes on endless staves of excitement
as he called everyone up to tell of a feeling
he feared was too good to contain.
Unable to describe it, he announced instead
that the earth was about to hatch a hesitant syllable:
the sound of a blue ship lost in a blue sea.

WATERWORKS

Space   to listen to Beethoven's deafness

Inciting peacefulness, primeval mornings
on whose advice
we are aloft for the weekend

And find, at the highest speed, quietude

And at the summit, a dalliance
where everything
              conspires to rain . . .

Elevations, shorelines
We started from sea level, with the debris of musicians

A life spent listening to yourself

                with the shells

your ear
against the sky
    (where each line on the page ends

   black murey, pink murey, hawk wings
   abalone, rose murex, white whelk

The conch shell since it let go of the rock,
    filled with the sound of flight

CODA

roll off you
    off a wave

(my heart felt hollow
        and strangely cool

And now, an understanding of fog
      of why clouds
          lie down to rest

A suggestion
        of magnitude

The cat walks in wondering where we are
Its tail a question mark

       In advance of silence,
no complaints

dream awhile scheme awhile

lay beside the wave that brought me here

BIG WOMAN HOLDING A PLUM

So she wasn't
   and sunning herself with countless grayhounds
curled up where she was stretched out
     riparian
relaxed, with the warmth of the rocks beneath her spine

Suppose she had one hand on a Panda's belly
and was polishing your badge with the other

Suppose she invented smoky quartz
and whenever she complained
the stream, with an irritating solicitude,
made little waves to hear her better

and brought down more fat and blissful admirers
(scrofulous churls, afloat on inner-tubes,
who made the charioteers groan
as they sponged down the flanks of their steeds)

Black Tulips! and you just stood there,
    gum sticking to the soles of your feet
and humming your country's anthem
with fragments of a broken mirror, particles
of something you couldn't arrange, a handful, like this.

Paul Violi's *In Baltic Circles*

by Matt Hart

I. Afterward Afterword

In 2008 I wrote a review of Paul Violi's book, *Overnight*, for *Coldfront Magazine*. Shortly after it appeared I was pleasantly surprised to receive an email from the poet himself, wherein, among other things, he asked for my address (I immediately sent it, of course—this guy was a giant to me! The only thing better would've been getting a transmission from Samuel Taylor Coleridge in the Vast—which, come to think of it, is exactly what hearing from Paul was like). A week later, a package arrived containing copies of Paul's books, a wonderful letter, and an early chapbook titled *Waterworks*. Weirdly, the package also contained a stack of legal-sized paper, binder-clipped together on one end, and backed with flimsy cardboard. On the left hand side of the top page was the following handwritten note:

> Dear Matt—I thought you might get a
> kick out of this—a photocopy of a book
> that's fallen apart & been scribbled on
> over a few decades. I like to think it's not
> all juvenilia! —Paul

The photocopied book was, as you may have guessed, *In Baltic Circles*, a book published by Kulchur Foundation in 1973 on the heels of three earlier chapbooks: *She'll Be Riding Six White Horses*, *Automatic Transmissions*, and (the aforementioned) *Waterworks*. But *In Baltic Circles* was Paul's first major collection (82 poems, 128 pages!) and, by the time he sent the photocopy to me, long out-of-print. Looking back on how we got to this point of reissue, it's funny to think that when *In Baltic Circles* originally appeared I was only three years old, and more than three decades later, looking at the book as Paul sent it to me with his many years of scrawl, edits, and revision—of wrestling with (and drawing on) what he'd done in that first BIG BOOK—I'm completely blown away by how contemporary the poems feel, how alive it all was and still is. Present tense.

One thought generating another
the momentum growing until the mind
spins sweetly like a top

(from "Idlewild")

What's more, before even reading all of the poems, I could tell what I had in front of me was NOT "juvenilia," but an unbelievably good "classic" Paul Violi book, the blueprint and foundation for everything that came after—the formal innovation/invention, the collision of surreal absurdity with Romantic description and declaration, the wordplay, the attention to music, the simultaneous reverence and indecorousness, the wild-at-heart violations of poetic decorum, the clash of high poetic diction with lowbrow words like "fatso" and "klutz," the comedy (stand up!), and the real human torque. It's all here, tentacles erudite, hilarious, and thrashing.

Judging by Paul's note above and the numerous handwritten marginal notes, edits, and rewrites in the photocopy, it's clear he came back to *In Baltic Circles* repeatedly, using it as a resource for working through his own ideas about what a Paul Violi poem might/should/could be:

> I've always wanted a map
> which changes as I follow it.

(from "Nicean")

For me, as a young(-ish) poet, seeing Paul's process was somehow heartening—it was a reminder that to write and publish poems is to engage in an activity (both creative and analytical) that doesn't necessarily end with the publication of a book. That poetry writing isn't necessarily about making a FINAL product, but about diving into a tradition of making art out of words. The best poems are the ones we continue to wrestle with, both as writers and readers. And considering that we change, in terms of experience and perspective, our sense of them may change over time as well. The idea that poets write books rather than poems, and that all of them (the books, the poems, and the poets) somehow arrive in the world airtight and sewn up for eternity, ready to win a contest (and be forgotten forever) is ludicrous. Poetry, as Paul well knew, will always resist finish, because poetic language isn't just employed in the service of particulars, it's deployed in the service of the infinite—the Vast and the Void and everything in between. And this fundamental slipperiness is what makes poetry, and Paul's poetry in particular, such a marvelous riot to engage with and re-engage with over and over again.

That said, for all the time Paul obviously spent with *In Baltic Circles*, it's important to point out that when it came to doing this reissue, he decided (and I certainly agree) that aside from making obvious corrections to mistakes in the original, the poems should, for the most part, appear as they did in 1973. This might seem a bit counterintuitive after all the talk about process/revision above, but it was Paul's constant re-ignition of his work (and the works of others—most especially perhaps the Romantics) that allowed him to keep producing (eleven more books of) new work. It's hard to remember sometimes that revising/editing poems isn't about fixing anything; it's about finding one's way forward to the poem at hand and also to new poems by thinking through choices already made.

> Think of all the Logicians,
> the righteous afternoons we spend
> watching their footprints evaporate around us
> and the extinct holidays that swirl
> over our heads at night like galaxies.
>
> In the morning, moths
> careening into the sun. No tiresome
> predictability, but progressions, and robins
> on the lawn that evolved into the number 5

(from "Aerial")

What was important was the deployment of the poems into the world in the first place. They became the basis for continued exploration and new discovery.

II. Public Works

It's truly great how Violi, from the very start (of this book and in some ways his poetic career too), begins reinventing both formally and in terms of content what a poem can be/contain—exploring possibilities and pushing against the constraints and decorum of poetic taste and tradition, often with hilarious and beautifully human results. And it's astonishing to me that somehow, even as a very young poet, Violi realized that poetry wants to be as big as the world, that nothing is off limits, and as a result there is no such thing as non-poetic language.

"Public Works," the poem that opens *In Baltic Circles*, begins with "Swinburne" (presumably Charles Algernon—who else?) pulling up to a light with

> …35 screeching yellow cabs.
> They rev their engines
> the light turns red
> they sound their horns
> And off they go.
>
> "Tally ho," yells Swinburne, "tally ho!"

"Red" means "go" here, and that in turn means the whole book (and by extension Violi's poetic career) begins with a traffic violation—and, one might add, with recklessness (35 cabs running a red light!), decadence (Swinburne!), noise (the horns! the engines!), and a double "Tally ho"—the traditional cry in a foxhunt to urge the hounds to action at first site of the fox.

Speaking of foxes (though first bid adieu to Mr. Swinburne as we won't see him again), enter Monet crossing the George Washington Bridge, not thinking about

> our first President's dentures.
> He could care less.
> He drives slowly up the Palisades.
> A flock of cabs passed him a long time ago.
> It's 11:63 a.m. and he could care less.
> It's a warm spring day
> and the bugs splatter like snowflakes
> against his windshield.
> Soon it is covered with the multi-colored splotches.

Clearly the poem gets weirder as it goes with the non-time 11:63 a.m., the repetition of "He could care less" (which feels like a deliberate, musical redundancy—a charmed/charming obliviousness), and finally the bugs splattering "like snowflakes"—quite an odd simile for a "warm spring day." Of course, the bug-splattered windshield, which Violi describes as "covered with multi-colored splotches," is suggestive of an impressionist painting (good thing Monet's driving!). Somehow all of this strikes me as a third-person version of a Frank O'Hara "I do this, I do that/Personal poem" (with O'Hara's "hum-colored cabs," frequent notation of the time, and references to his friends and art). But in "Public Works," rather than "I do this, I do that" it's "they do this" and "he does that," and all of it's sort of wrong. Not to mention that the New York City SCENE of many of Frank O'Hara's poems has here been traded for SCENERY—the George Washington Bridge and the Palisades Parkway. But I digress.

Just when the poem seems like it might start spinning its wheels, Monet "stops for gas," and "When the attendant begins to clean the windshield," Monet, "can do one of two things: he either...."

No, that's not a mistake. That's where the stanza breaks, but rather than continuing on in the next stanza with Monet's choice we get an interruption—a screeching dis-enjambment into a parenthetical—a pop-up window advertisement in the middle of the poem:

> (Hi, I'm Paul Violi and I'd like a word with you
> about BIC pens. I've written some swell poems
> with BIC pens and so has my wife, Ann. I expect
> our child will really like BIC pens too. You know
> how ordinary pens sometimes botch things up and
> give you a glimpse of things to come like, well,
> when I'm old and getting a bit, uh, senile, I suppose
> my mind, like yours, neighbor, will skip a word
> here and there, scratch a mere impression of what
> should have been a fine thought on the page and,
> in a manner of speaking, just plain run out of ink.
> But there is no reason your pen has to falter like
> that and you can bet BIC pens never will. So take
> my advice, do yourself a favor and buy a BIC pen
> today. Pick up a couple for the whole family while
> you're at it and tell them I sent you!)

Enter: Paul Violi. And what is it he's doing? Pitching BIC pens, scratching "a mere impression of what should have been a fine thought on the page"—which ironically makes it an amazingly fine thought. It's as if Violi erects (and how disruptively/eruptively) a billboard right in the public space of the poem—buying some time, selling some pens, publicly introducing himself as poet.

This commercial/pop-up window begs us to pay all of our attention to the man behind the curtain, his wife, his child, the pens he uses (he's using) to write his poems. Don't forget, however, as you're reading the billboard to keep your eyes on the road, too. Violi's poems require us to multi-task as we read, to pay attention to the layers of meaning, the ways that poetry radiates (rather than delineates) the past and the present and the future all at once. The funny thing is that (thus far anyway) the public "works" in question aren't, for example, highbrow public sculpture or even civil construction projects. They're traffic violations and ad campaign testimonials. It's bad poetic behavior in public— which is hilarious, but also really smart in the way it sets up expectations Violi later undermines.

Thus, a commercial, an index, a police blotter could be just as legitimate poetically as a sonnet or a pastoral or an epic written in *terza rima*. His toolbox of poetic approaches and devices are so layered, that poem by poem, book by book, he was able to draw on and invent constraints for writing that other poets with a more limited toolbox (and that's pretty much everybody) couldn't even begin to imagine. His is a poetry of wonder and wander, of marvelous craftsmanship and constant invention and re-invention, a poetics where, as he puts it in his poem "Boredom,"—a poem where he essentially builds a factory, just to set it on fire—"There is no lighting problem here." Everything is potentially illuminated, there is always someplace new to locate (light) oneself, and the spark (if one is bright enough and brave enough to follow it) always seemingly leads to a fire.

But what of the rest of "Public Works"? Well, after the parenthetical, the poem picks up this way:

> It's still a warm spring day
> and a man waving
> a square orange flag
> diverts Monet into the outer lane.

Notice that Monet's choice is completely out of the picture. "It's still a warm spring day" but things have changed. Monet is no longer at the gas station, and, well, it's a new stanza, a new era—no reason to cry over splattered bugs, or Impressionism or anything else. The parenthetical, it turns out, was both a roadblock and a detour that once we move through it spits us out somewhere not entirely familiar, near where we need to be, but not where we would've gotten otherwise. And isn't that what happens in the poetic process? One picks up a pen or starts typing, starts driving, and it's never really clear where/how we'll go, because often it isn't very clear what we're driving at. So we keep shifting gears, and sometimes we go from first to second, but either due to a mistake or a mechanical error (a slip in the transmission), we go from first into fourth or neutral, or reverse.

All this shifting attention diverts Monet into the outer lanes (the margins) of the poem. So much for Monet, as now he disappears from view, but Violi keeps going and this is important. Essentially what's happening and what's been happening all along is that he's giving us a look at the creative process—his creative process—by making the gear shifts and mental leaps a part of the poem, i.e., he's presenting the actual work publicly, rather than making something that's all buttoned up and too tidy to breathe.

Here we get the breaks, the tears, the way forward, and also all the old junked ideas abandoned on the roadside. This not only makes for an excellent demonstration of the choices Violi's making (because they're so extreme), but for a really dynamic—if somewhat herky-jerky—structure.

I can imagine someone at this point saying, "Yeah, that's all fine and good. But where's the gravity, the human torque you mentioned earlier?" Well hang on.

After Monet is diverted into the outer lanes of the poem by the man waving "a square orange flag" (an image that strikes me more like a guy waving a Mark Rothko painting around than a flag) the poem's speaker (not Violi—who has clearly differentiated himself from the speaker earlier in the poem—"Hi, I'm Paul Violi") describes men painting lines and fixing cracks in the road:

> Other men in red vests
> have placed orange stanchions in the road,
> another drives a blue truck at 3 miles per hour.
> They follow him on foot, spraying white lines
> and double white lines, yellow lines
> and broken yellow lines while 3 men in black boots
> chop up shiny casks of tar, melt it
> and scribble the stuff over the cracks
> in the pavement.
> The gray concrete sparkles and its reflection hovers
> over it like a mirage on the wrong road to wonderland.

The last two lines of this stanza are so off-kilter beautiful that I almost can't stand it. On the one hand, Violi seems to be describing the heat-mirage-haze that hangs above the pavement on a warm day, especially where men are working and the exhaust from the cars mixes with light. However, ending the stanza with "the wrong road to wonderland" is so perfect here, as we've been on a bunch of "wrong" roads in the course of the poem, and yet they do in fact lead to a kind of wonderland of association and exploration—four pages later in this reading, and just look how far we've come from the poem's initial lawlessness at the red light. The poet's writing lines (of various stripes), the workers are painting lines of various stripes, and notice all the colors: red, orange, blue, white, yellow, black, gray, and the scribbling of the tar over the cracks. The stanza is an action painting, a real Jackson Pollock! And these public workers are artists as much as anybody. The poem continues:

> The first to eat lunch
> wipes his hands on a green t-shirt.
> He steps off the road and examines a tomato
> and cheese sandwich: "... I remember a job
> we did near the shore, a parking lot.
> My brother Harry worked that one.
> So did my cousin and my nephew.
> We laid down about an acre of asphalt
> near the beach and I used to take my daughter
> there at odd hours for driving lessons.

From here, the worker continues to speak, and we'll get to more of what he says in a moment. But first, I love how he "steps off the road" before he starts talking, like an actor stepping off the main part of the stage with a couple of props (here a "tomato" and a "cheese sandwich") to deliver a soliloquy directly and intimately to the audience. And the story he tells is personal, about work and family—a simple story and compelling because of it. In this is the notion that sometimes the poem we're writing/reading is the poem we're finding in the margins—the one just off the beaten track a bit, where one least expects it. The worker continues:

> I explained to her how we had put down
> a long white line and then angling into that one
> a lot of short, slanted ones.
> But she said it looked like the skeleton of a fish.
> I couldn't teach her anything.
> She lives in the city now. I think she's married.
>
> But in summer, it's packed on Sundays
> and let me tell you something: when I see all the spaces
> filled and the cars glittering like a fish on its side
> in the sunlight, I want to tell you
> it's no accident. I'm glad my brother convinced me
> to take this job. It ain't all politics."

I'm struck with such incredible sadness by "I couldn't teach her anything. / She lives in the city. I think she's married." Suddenly the poem has a black hole, one that can't be covered over with paint or asphalt. Then, the worker simply returns to talk about the parking lot and being glad about his job. He thinks his daughter is married, but he doesn't know? This feels tragic—the father disconnected from his daughter in this way. The power here is in what he doesn't say, which is a brilliant move on Violi's part. It's as if the worker begins to talk about himself, his private life, and then realizes he's giving up too much. He's at work. He's speaking out loud about personal things in public.

The way this poem wears its process on its sleeve could be described in terms similar to those the worker uses to describe both the asphalt and the lines they painted on it. One writes a line, and then a bunch of other lines, some words come together, others fall away. Often at first it doesn't read like much or maybe it reads like a dead thing ("the skeleton of a fish"), but possibly that's because one isn't looking at it the right way (with the right attention), and once we figure out how to look at it, it becomes something full of possibility, beauty, and terror.

And the worker's right about another thing: "It's no accident." Everything in this poem is deliberate, but so strangely assembled it might seem sloppy or just plain bizarre to the casual reader. What I'm demonstrating here are the rewards one gets reading Violi slowly, acrobatically, with attention to the poems in terms of what they say and how they say it, microscopically and macroscopically, topsy-turvy, inside out.

As we near the end of "Public Works", and this reading,

> The rest of the men unpack their lunches.
> Some exchange sandwiches, some of them drink orange
> soda, others guzzle grape juice or beer.
>
> The second crew has finished shoveling asphalt
> off the back of the truck.
> The paint is still drying,
> all the holes in the road are now bumps.

Somehow "Public Works" works because of "all the holes in the road"—the poem winds up amounting to both more than, and at the same time exactly, the sum of its parts. It's an auspicious beginning to a book that's chock full of surprises, that on every page undermines and sometimes obliterates expectations with amazing clarity and openness, ridiculously with so much grace. This book is a great treasure that we're lucky to see back in print.

III. The Vast and The Void

Unfortunately, after we started work on this reissue, Paul was diagnosed with pancreatic cancer and passed away in April 2011, before we could see the book back into print. With that in mind, and to be absolutely clear, the idea isn't really to have a last (afterword) word here, but to help ensure Paul's words last and put them into the hands of as large an audience as possible.

For those of us already familiar with his work, including his legions of devoted former students, it's clear and crucial: Paul Violi needs to be read (and taught) MORE—with incredible seriousness and with serious delight. He was, hands down, one of our best poets—inventive, original, adventurous, and resourceful—his poems always pushing the boundaries and expanding the possibilities of what poetry *could* be, while simultaneously reaffirming at every instant exactly what poetry has always been: singing in the service of the infinite.

Notice

This elevator is not working today.
Just consider it an anonymous eulogy.

Please use the 53ʳᵈ Street entrance.
Thank you for your cooperation—

The Management

(from "Excerpts from The Chronicles")

H_NGM_N BKS Reissues seek to honor the individual volume as the ultimate realization of a writer's vision, republishing out of print or scarce volumes judged to be essential to our contemporary conversations of poetics/ aesthetics.